Visions for the Future,
Learning from the Past

Reconciliation

THE PROPHETIC ROLE OF

GLASTONBURY

James Turnbull

Though I speak with the tongues
of men and of angels,
and have not Love,
I am become as sounding brass,
or a tinkling cymbal.
And though I have
the gift of prophecy,
and understand all mysteries,
and all knowledge;
and though I have all faith,
so that I could remove mountains,
and have not Love, I am nothing.

Love suffereth long, and is
kind;
Love envieth not;
Love vaunteth not itself,
is not puffed up,
doth not behave itself
unseemly,
seeketh not her own,
is not easily provoked,
thinketh no evil;
rejoiceth not in iniquity,
but rejoiceth in the truth.

(1 Corinthians 13)

The
Prophetic Role
of Glastonbury

TO BE A BLESSING FOR THE WORLD

James Turnbull

*with foreword by Ray Simpson of Lindisfarne
and a brief biography*

**Abbey Press
Glastonbury**

2001

The Prophetic Role of Glastonbury

Copyright © 2001 Rosemary Turnbull and Catherine van den Bosch

Cover panorama of Glastonbury,
from the Holy Thorn on Wearyall Hill,
by Liz Beech of the Phoenix Project

Photo of James on back cover courtesy of
Third Eye Films, Glastonbury

Pictish bull in knotwork (page 173) and cross (page 176)
by Mark Olly, from his book *Celtic Warrington;*
All other Celtic decorations from The Datafile, Weston-super-Mare

Designed and set in 10-point EFF Bristol (Minister),
headings in Lothlorian, on Acorn workstations,
by Abbey Press

Printed and bound in Great Britain
by Micro Laser Designs, Bath,
using environment-friendly paper

Abbey Press
32 Norbins Road, Glastonbury, Somerset, BA6 9JG
www.abbeypress.net   turnbull @ abbeypress.net

A catalogue record for this book is available from the British Library

ISBN 0-9533203-2-4

Foreword

by Ray Simpson
Guardian of the Community of Aidan and Hilda, Lindisfarne

James Turnbull is a prophet who stands at the crossroads of a new age. He points to new spiritual energies which we must take seriously. He points out the misuse of power in the Christian Church which obscures its *raison d'être* and which it must now leave behind. Although he understands why so many good people have jettisoned the Church in favour of less restrictive spiritualities, he is aware that these, too, can be prey to egocentric takeover.

So, from Glastonbury, a world arena of ancient and modern spiritualities, he calls us to develop a grounding in adequate spiritual disciplines. He sees in the Celtic Christian tradition a way to sift the spirits, to harness that which is eternally true in the Christian Faith to that which is true in natural sciences and other spiritualities.

I count it a privilege to have shared something of James's vision towards the end of his life. He is a courageous and wise spiritual guide whose insights are worthy of deep refection. The challenges he articulates in this book provide us with an agenda for the rest of our lives; they take us into the new age of the spirit.

Contents

7

Introduction

James Turnbull wrote these fourteen annual Newsletters between 1984 and 1998. They talk about how Glastonbury evolved during those years. He is deeply concerned with the historical background to the reasons why the Church has ended up where it is today. He shows the possibilities that Glastonbury holds to be a wonderful blessing for the world, if we learn to work together to build bridges between denominations, religions and "new age" thinking. The Newsletters seem even more relevant now than when they were written.

Visions for the future — learning from the past. That phrase sums up James's approach. He specially drew inspiration from the early Celtic Christian Church, with its insights into healing and wholeness and its caring relationship with the Earth, nature, creation and each other.

We have done very little to change his original text, other than to add punctuation [and a very few notes]. We felt that if we began to edit the Newsletters it would alter the uniqueness of James's style. But it must be remembered that each Newsletter was written for that year; they were not intended to be read one immediately after the other. James weaves many different threads together, so there may appear to be some repetition.

As people who knew James will know, everything he says comes out of a genuine love of people. Jesus was always his example. He would not ignore the truth, because it is only through truth that we can find truth, but love and wisdom go hand in hand to make the truth acceptable for those who are willing to hear.

James often refers to "the Alternatives". This was his term for the many people attracted to Glastonbury who seek a new approach to the meaning of religion, who thoroughly question traditional values but often hold a special love for Jesus Christ in their hearts though they find it difficult to express this within the conventional framework of the Church.

James's understanding for the more mystical side of the Christian Way gave him a deep sense of the prophetic in everyday life. He became a trusted spiritual guide to seekers and leaders in all walks of life. An obituary in the local newspaper called him "honorary godfather to half of Glastonbury."

There is a holly tree at the east end of the Abbey grounds dedicated to James. Its evergreen leaves reflect the light and its colourful berries lift our spirits in winter when all seems dark. Our ancestors considered the holly so sacred that they renamed it the "holy tree" or "Christ's thorn".

We hope that all readers find the Newsletters in this collected form helpful and illuminating, and that they will give us all encouragement to move forward, leaving past hurts behind so that we can build the foundations of something new and meaningful for us all as we enter the twenty-first century.

Catherine (Turnbull) van den Bosch
Rosemary Turnbull

Glastonbury, 3 November 2001

Warm thanks to Jim Nagel at Abbey Press, Liz Beech at the Phoenix Project, Maxie Lavaulx, Pamela Bellars, Ray Simpson and Alardus van den Bosch for their support, advice, hard work and patience, without which this book would never happened.

December 1984

First Glastonbury Newsletter

Arrival in Glastonbury

It is now more than four years since we made a venture of faith and moved to 34 Hood Close, Glastonbury. We came, without a definite priestly ministry for James, in part to follow the late Marjorie Milne of 21 Manor House Road, a woman of prayer to whom God revealed that Glastonbury should become a focal point for national and international reconciliation. More than 400 years after the dissolution of the great medieval Abbey, the crypt under the Lady Chapel and St Patrick's chapel where Marjorie prayed is once again a centre for regular worship — but there is a long way to go before her vision is fulfilled.

After a short honeymoon period, as no job emerged and some opposition did, James registered unemployed; this provided an opportunity to take stock of the situation. As any soldier knows, time spent in reconnaissance is seldom wasted; in the West Country it is wise to move slowly and let the purposes of God unfold. God made man in Jesus Christ is the Master of Time and plans true spiritual warfare. His is the victory, not ours.

Past history of Glastonbury

The past history of Glastonbury has been one of intermittent periods of ascent to spiritual heights followed by plunges into the depths. It has been and still is a place of conflict between natural and spiritual forces which can give rise to great creative potential when tensions are resolved, or to warring factions when they are not. Glastonbury is a meeting point for pre-Christian religions including Hebrew and Indo-European Celtic faiths as well as Orthodox Celtic (Irish as well as British or Welsh), Anglo-Saxon, Norman and Roman, Christian forms. Many people who have come here in recent years believe they have been called here by God; some are given to illusion, others are exploring new avenues of spirituality or opening up old ones with little or no concern for holiness.

There was division between the rich and powerful Abbey and its supporters and poor pilgrims and ordinary people of the town before the first Reformation. Since the judicial murder of the last abbot and two of his monks on top of the Tor during 1539 there has been no focal point for agreement and, even before that, agreement was imposed from above; such agreement is illusion.

The position was not helped by national and international sectarian quarrels, especially those of the late 19th and early 20th centuries. Not surprisingly, many local people see the various invasions of "newcomers" which began in earnest nearly 100 years ago as irrelevant to, or as a threat to, their way of life; many still carry on a life of their own. Today Glastonbury is a microcosm of social and religious divisions which affect Britain and Ireland. Like Jerusalem in the Holy Land, it is a place intended by God to be the "possession of peace" which has not yet attained its destiny. The issues which have to be faced in love and charity before this can happen are deep and need to be handled with care. Marjorie Milne as a historian with a profound spirituality and prayer life was ahead of her time in seeing the potential of Glastonbury at a critical time in

Glastonbury is a microcosm of social and religious divisions which affect Britain and Ireland

the life of our nation and the world. Many regard us as living at the end of an age, and the Church cannot yet provide an effective meeting point for the whole community.

Roots of schism

We in Britain have lost our role at the centre of a great Empire which withstood the might of the fascist Roman Empire and its successors in western Europe. We have combined high ideals with naked self-interest leading to economic exploitation, abuse of power and some atrocities. Like other nations we spend vast sums on defence and yet cannot reconcile inner conflicts between the south, with its control of finance from London, and the north, where live the industrial workers who provide much of our wealth. These and other visible expressions of division have deep hidden roots which stem from our past. Perhaps the key to resolve them is to be found in Glastonbury in the spiritual search for the Grail.

> Our divisions have deep hidden roots in our past — perhaps the key to resolve them is found in Glastonbury

Glastonbury reminds us that Christianity in these islands derives in the first place from the Middle East, from Hebrew, Greek and Egyptian sources, commencing in AD45 with Bishop Aristobulus if not earlier. Later the diocesan system of Church government linked to the State gave bishops vast tracts of territory; it was imposed on the whole Church following the Council of Nicaea and the arrival of St Augustine in AD597. It could never embrace the whole of the spiritual life of these islands, even if through history it has been the most powerful form. The roots of many of our schisms are still expressed outwardly as power struggles between Roman and Anglican forms of spirituality, between warring factions in the Church of England expressed in its General Synod, and the Free Churches which reject this form of centralized control. In addition there are hidden political, cultural and economic factors in division which are of as much consequence as the "theological" ones; to disregard them is to cut off the Church from daily life and to perpetuate disunity between the churches at a time when a new spiritual consciousness is emerging apart from the churches themselves.

Misuse of power has given rise to mutual condemnation of one's opponents as satanic, even if this is not openly expressed in words. If we cannot silence our opponents by superior rational arguments we ridicule or insult them and, if this doesn't work, we bring them under control with the help of riot police, force of arms, or — in extremis — by inquisition; thus when communication breaks down and money is required for defence or war it can lead to violence in our streets or, in a previous generation, to the destruction of the Abbey. Added to this is our unsatisfactory relationship with nature and the land, with which Marjorie Milne became concerned towards the end of her life as she sought to hammer out what makes for reconciliation.

Current response by the churches

So far this letter has stated an outline of the problem we face both nationally and locally at a time when thousands upon thousands of people pour into Glastonbury each year, some seeking spiritual answers and finding little if any spiritual food in our churches. They include Roman Catholics, Anglicans, Orthodox, Free Church, charismatic fellowships, Israelites, Druids, Essenes, natural occultist and spiritist healers, astrologers, CND supporters, Hare Krishna devotees, some part-Christian, unemployed people or drifters, pilgrims from many lands, each bringing his own idea of spirituality including some "leaders" who build up separatist groups, often of young people. As TV programmes bear witness, the initiative lies mainly with those on the fringes or outside of Church life.

Butchering 'infidels' and persecuting 'heretics': western Europe has to grow up

In reflection, it is not surprising that the Church is wallowing in Glastonbury as it is elsewhere in the country; no doubt it was doing so in medieval times when Glastonbury was a great centre of pilgrimage after the Crusades when "Christians" had been thrown out of the Holy Land following Arab and Turkish "Holy Wars" against western European imperialism. Inevitably this gave rise to power struggles. Then as now other faiths were brought into this country, and butchering of "infidels" gave way to persecution of "heretics". Western Europe now has to grow up.

14

Some activities of the Turnbulls

Since they moved to Glastonbury, God has not been inactive in the lives of the Turnbulls. After the initial check, a door opened for James to operate in relation to the Christian healing ministry in the southwest. By joining the Mothers' Union at both St John's and St Benedict's (the two Anglican churches) and various Bible-study and prayer groups Rosemary was able to work behind the scenes to support the clergy and the Council of Churches to try to bring Christians together. An interregnum at St Benedict's from January 1982 provided more of an opportunity for James to relate to local people as well as to those alienated from the Church. By August 1982, after some months of living by faith, financial problems which had been fairly acute were largely resolved.

The annual day of reconciliation on August 6th first begun by Marjorie Milne in 1975 continued. [The date is both the feast of the Transfiguration of Jesus and of the atomic bomb on Hiroshima.] Teaching days related to the Christian healing ministry began in Somerset and activities were expanded in Dorset, Devon and Avon. Thanks to a number of people, especially Brian Frost, Mary Miller, May Valentine and Jean Smith, it was possible to reach out in a number of directions including to those on the fringe of Church life and to people who are socially deprived.

August 6th as annual day of reconciliation: Transfiguration and atomic bomb

Greenlands

A year before the arrival of the Turnbulls, Jim Nagel, who also knew Marjorie Milne, had — in conjunction with Mrs Alison Collyer — begun an experiment in community living related to the land at Greenlands Farm, Wick, on the outskirts of Glastonbury. This soon ran into many difficulties but for five years has provided an open door for all kinds of people, many in deep trouble, who came to Glastonbury. Jim left the "community" in December 1982 when he married his wife Viola; they now have a son; Jim has become a teacher with a concern for "pilgrims". Alison, who has faced many crises with great courage and endurance, has reached agreement for the farm to be purchased by a group from North Paddington, London, who have brought into being a charitable trust concerned with reconciliation between town and country, and are also willing to accept the kind of farming and care of animals and land in which Alison believes. The Trust is already making a significant contribution to what is still a daunting task; backing has been received from charities and private individuals including the British Council of Churches, but there are formidable obstacles to be overcome.

Nevertheless something has been happening at Greenlands from which the churches have much to learn. **Reconciliation is false if it does not take into account those who are not "respectable middle class"**. If a "New Abbey" is eventually to emerge in Glastonbury, what can be learnt from Greenlands Farm, the Assembly Rooms, the Glastonbury Experience and the Gothic Image needs to be taken into account, for without this the Church cannot be brought back into the mainstream of life.

The way forward

To meet the situation, the first need to emerge is for more prayer on the part of Christians in Glastonbury, coupled with more awareness of the possibilities both in the town and nationally. A move forward was made with the cooperation of the Council of Churches in 1983 when, following a suggestion from Rosemary, an ecumenical prayer group came into being which visits each church in turn. More prayer and study groups are coming into being, giving hope for the future.

On the wider scene a link-up with Bishop Morris Maddocks and the "Acorn Apostolate", in which both James and Rosemary are involved, as well as James's membership of the Guild of Health council, gives hope of more doctor–clergy cooperation and growth in the Christian healing ministry. James is also a member in an ecumenical capacity of the Bath and Wells diocesan Healing Advisory Group.

From Ammerdown and Lord Hylton comes awareness of how the Church can play a role in bridging some of the social and cultural divisions in our country, in part by drawing upon experience of our fellow Christians in Ireland which has ancient links with Glastonbury. James has also become a trustee of the Grail Trust, involved with a centre for prayer and modern spirituality at Stoke St Gregory, halfway between Glastonbury and Taunton.

In the long run more contact between Glastonbury and religious orders and communities such as Benedictines and Franciscans (not excluding Mirfield) and newer communities and missionary societies could attract prayer and other support as growing awareness of possibilities penetrates the denominational structures of the Church. At the right time, as Marjorie Milne foresaw, this could lead to the formation of an ecumenical community of reconciliation in or near Glastonbury related to the land with a "sound" Christ-centred spiritual discipline. During the Middle Ages this function was carried out by the International Order of Hospitallers. A "Hospitallers of St David" group has already come into being at St David's in Wales, stemming in part from Marjorie Milne. The members have a concern for learning from Celtic and Orthodox as well as "Catholic" spirituality. The aim is to care for pilgrims to St David's, for young people including the poor, the homeless, the sick and the spiritually hungry. Maybe such a body could help us recover more of our deep spiritual roots and fulfil a need in Glastonbury and all over Britain, linking up with Christians in Ireland and beyond, but that is beyond the scope of this letter.

... an ecumenical community of reconciliation at Glastonbury related to the land

December 1985

Second Glastonbury Newsletter

The hidden power of the past

Seen against the background of eternity, five years, the length of time the Turnbulls have been in Glastonbury, is a very short time. It is also a short time to come to grips with the natural powers, spiritual currents, undercurrents and cross-currents, to say nothing of political and economic complications and enmities, which for centuries have prevented Glastonbury from playing an effective role in national and international reconciliation. Such "principalities and powers" snarl up attempts to proclaim the Christian faith here, and it is scarcely surprising that those who have lived here for generations, including churchgoers, have carved out a life with scant regard for the hidden power which the past exercises over the present; ghosts from the past, like sleeping dogs, may bite when roused!

In the main, people who come from outside Glastonbury may stir things up; many who do are not Christians. When this is done without learning enough from those who live here, and about past conflicts, action is taken without an adequate spiritual base and this leads to more conflict. Examples include what happened to Bligh Bond, the architect engaged to help restore the Abbey more than seventy years ago who became involved with spiritualism, and to Rutland Boughton the "left-winger", and others, who sought to develop a centre for the arts in Glastonbury, or events which led to a revived interest in astrology.

Fear and guilt means that what should be a tremendously creative place fails to fulfil its role, and the Church becomes divorced from the spiritual aspirations of people who see Glastonbury as the "New Jerusalem" of both British and world significance. As we move into the "New Age" we live at a time of growing world crisis, growing rate of change, a change of consciousness for which the Church is almost totally unprepared. Thus much of the search for spirituality goes on outside of the Church although Glastonbury has Christian roots deep in our history which could give hope for the future if we are prepared to explore them.

Roots of new spirituality in Glastonbury

Long before the arrival of the "Culdees" (Christian and other refugees from the eastern Mediterranean and the Holy Land) in Glastonbury and elsewhere in Britain and Ireland, changes followed the arrival of the megalithic peoples who built Stonehenge and other stone circles, and the "beaker" people or shepherds from the Middle East who came here before the Celts brought high civilization and druidical priesthood. In this area lies a common spirituality and our Indo-European ancestry. Traces remain of a connection between Druids and Old Testament spirituality which the Roman Empire did not entirely wipe out in spite of ruthless attempts to suppress truth. Later the Celtic Church (which by around AD45 had been led by Bishop Aristobulus, one of the seventy, a Cypriot) suffered much during the Diocletian persecution around AD300.

200 years later Augustine came to Canterbury to coerce reluctant Celts into Latin conformity

Then came the crucial conflict with Martin of Tours when the Roman Emperor, supported by wealthy power-oriented bishops, began persecuting "heretics", some of whom the poor and powerless would regard as true Saints. Some two hundred years later St Augustine came to Canterbury seeking to coerce reluctant Celts into Latin conformity. The policy continued when St Dunstan introduced Benedictine instead of Celtic spirituality at Glastonbury and opposed the married state of the clergy. Gradually the Church lost much of its hold on Christian truth and it is not surprising that after the Norman conquest an abbot butchered some of the Saxon monks who opposed him.

Inevitably, during the Middle Ages the Benedictine movement became corrupted by power and wealth; in AD1539 Abbot Whiting, who refused to surrender Church wealth to the grasping hand of an impoverished King and State, became martyr in the power struggle between the English Crown and Papacy, between Anglo-Norman Britain and much of western Europe. From the time of Constantine the Great in AD325, Church–State combinations led to Christian acquiescence to reigns of terror; the Church neglected its prophetic role. In Glastonbury, as in Britain, the Church divided into warring sections; theology ceased to be the queen of sciences as Christians, instead of loving one another, cursed not only enemies outside of the Church but warred against and cursed each other, losing sight of the Kingdom and rule of God, preferring national idolatry to the victory of good over evil. The Cross became the sign and symbol of self-sacrifice coupled with national aggression; groups sought power based on their beliefs and corrupted the Church, taking the name of God in vain.

Church–State combinations led to acquiescence in reigns of terror and losing its prophetic role

There followed the rise of the British Empire, war and civil war; in the 17th century the Quakers (who still have a strong community locally) began as a prophetic renewal movement, but felt compelled to reject the sacraments (like the Salvation Army two centuries later) which had been used to enforce priestly domination over "ordinary" people with backing from the State. This means that present-day divisions are as much political and economic as "theological", and the rise of atheism has some of its roots in opposition to the fascist system which manipulates bishops into key positions provided they serve

Mammon and not God. No wonder there have been power struggles between Roman Catholics and Anglicans and with the "Free Churches". Such struggles in the late 19th and early 20th century have left us with a legacy in Glastonbury still unresolved. The lobbying in the General Synod of the Church of England suggests that even now Anglicans have far from learnt their lesson; younger people, disgusted with the history and current behaviour of the churches, opt out and, according to some, revert to paganism. Church unity which does not take these factors into account is illusion. A spiritual revolution is needed within the Church of God. We need to learn to draw on Celtic as well as Benedictine insights, learning from, rather than rejecting, the fringe.

Celtic Christian spirituality learnt much from the Druids and from the East; it allows for speculation and adventure rather than seeking to contain the truth within rigid forms; it is not afraid of paradox. This more open spirituality is dangerous for some and raises questions about the role of astrology, psychic truth, male–female relationships, spiritualism and the Communion of Saints, natural creation, the underprivileged and the poor. Such a spirituality would be opposed to the desire to control everything from one world centre in Rome and is likely to have strands opposed to the European Economic Community and in favour of the Commonwealth of Nations. It need not deny that Rome is a centre of world significance but values the role of the Royal Family and especially the Crown as the "Defender of the Faith". It is likely to be feared by those who regard their own insights as having a monopoly of truth and desire to impose their beliefs on the whole Church. For its followers it means loving and forgiving even one's enemies unconditionally, seeking to bring peace and unity and the power to resolve conflicts not only within Glastonbury, but in our inner cities, in Northern Ireland, and the world; it means avoiding abuse of power.

Britain and the world need this kind of spirituality which respects the unorthodox and those on the fringe. One "fringe"

> Open Celtic spirituality allows for speculation and adventure rather than containing truth in rigid forms

example here in Glastonbury which has strengths and weaknesses is the British Israelite movement with its headquarters here. Once a powerful movement, its members see Britain as having a world role different from that of Rome, both as regards past history and spiritual destiny. When such a movement links up with extremists of the right wing, and with the aggressive nationalistic strain in the Old Testament, which sees Northern Ireland as a promised land given to Ulster Protestants, as the Holy Land was given to the successors of Moses, it becomes incompatible with Christianity of the more flexible kind associated with the Church of England and the British Royal Family. If Glastonbury is to fulfil an effective future role there is need for fusing Celtic, Franciscan and Benedictine spirituality, making for creative tension between order and freedom; such paradoxical insights are reconciled in the light of the Cross. We need Israelites like Nathaniel, who do not seek for power and are without guile.

... creative tension between order and freedom — paradoxes are reconciled in the light of the Cross

Current response of Glastonbury churches

The churches in Glastonbury are learning to pray with each other, and some share in joint "healing" services. The spiritual meeting point comes at the local level when we share in each other's pain at the foot of the Cross. This transcends barriers between denominations, between long-term residents and newcomers, between those with power and wealth and those without, between employed and unemployed, between townspeople and hippies or travellers, between church people and those outside of the Church who seek for truth even in occult areas which are destructive for some, who should avoid them like the plague lest they need deliverance from hidden powers.

Those who merely condemn the occult, or keep themselves to themselves, may become members of ingrown cliques, self-righteous and judgemental of "dirty hippies" evicted from Molesworth or Stonehenge or from sites in Wiltshire, Wales or Cornwall, whence came more than 300 dwellers in coaches, caravans or "benders" during 1985. Some were anarchistic or politically left-wing and arrived at a time when difficulties emerged in implementing the agreement reached during December 1984 between Mrs Collyer of Greenlands Farm (whom some would say has been a fool for Christ's sake) and the Paddington Farm Trust. Some in the town reach out, others react with suspicion, hatred and fear and even threaten violence. All the churches are affected by attitudes and beliefs which have national and international ramifications as well as affecting local trade and the community. No wonder many wish such a situation would go away.

Nevertheless, Glastonbury cannot opt out of her destiny. She attracts, and will continue to attract, worldwide interest, as what was once called the "Second Rome" is seen, as it was in the Middle Ages related to the cult of Joseph of Arimathea, as the "New Jerusalem", the spiritual heart not just of Britain but of the whole world in the "New Age" which is coming. Many in the churches (including some clergy and ministers) do not believe this to be true; some both within and outside of the Church believe in it. There is need to beware because behind the scenes are those deep into occult forces in finance and politics who seek ego-centric power; their tentacles reach into Glastonbury life; others who talk about the Cosmic Christ may be naive as they seek for truth at a time when some people openly try to reactivate natural and magical forces now that laws against witchcraft have been repealed.

> Glastonbury cannot opt out of her destiny — she continues to attract worldwide interest

Whether she likes it or not, the Church is presented with a growing challenge as some seek to break free of past limitations in western European thought; we have to face this challenge if the way is to be paved for profound spiritual renewal. Inevitable fears and suspicions of cults, of fringe alternative spirituality and astrology give rise to touchiness and at times near-hysteria on both sides of the divide between "orthodox" Christians and others. During 1985 opposition to a "living astrology" camp made it difficult for the organizers to find a farmer within miles of Glastonbury who would allow his land to be used by some

250 people during August. As many younger people have left conventional denominations to join such ventures because of the "deadness" of the churches, accusation and counter-accusation flourish. Some would add that this is aggravated when a Christian fellowship sets up its own church and begins to develop a deliverance ministry not given attention by the other churches. On the one hand this provides joy and fellowship lacking elsewhere, on the other it becomes open in condemnation of alternative spirituality, knowing little or nothing about it.

In all this and more, Glastonbury is a microcosm reflecting what happens in other places. To add to the spiritual confusion there is now an Eastern Orthodox Christian presence reminding us of the divisions between Latin, Greek and Anglican spirituality, between East and West. Younger people ask "Who is right?" and are confused and sceptical about the Church. Some believe in the Incarnation, Cross and Resurrection; others dismiss religion altogether or claim to be Christian whilst rejecting Christian morality and the Church's ministry.

Spiritual muddle

Not surprisingly in the midst of this muddle, some who come here get into the grips of powers and deceiving spirits which future priests and ministers are not taught to handle in theological colleges or parishes. Some need deliverance but turn to medicine or go it on their own; others talk about "higher consciousness" and the "New Age" believing that all light — even Lucifer — is of God, and that Satan is a figment of the imagination. This makes Glastonbury a place for dreams, illusions and self-deception rather than for spiritual discernment and genuine revelations of reality. There is need for a firm, soundly based spirituality so that the Church can learn to handle the diverse forces and currents here at a time when a growing number of young and spiritually immature people are practising natural means of healing, including reliving the past back to birth or

24

before-birth experiences even to "previous lives". Some practise spiritism, a few black magic, a few are Rosicrucians or adherents of Findhorn in Scotland, whence come people who "astral-travel" down the ley line which they believe joins Glastonbury to the Highlands of Scotland. Through all this and more confusion and deception people seek or do not seek the one true God and the person of Jesus Christ at a time when no proper provision is made to prepare parish clergy and ministers to meet such a spiritual challenge. If those who teach theology are unaware of these deeper levels, the Church has no Gospel to provide food for spiritually hungry people, who are often victims of spiritual warfare which the churches are not trained to fight.

The shape of things to come

For the future the need is for spiritual awareness, not mental knowledge; it stands out a mile that there is no way forward which is not based on a life of prayer and an adequate spiritual discipline, and that papering over the cracks which divide existing denominational structures will not overcome disunity, let alone resolve tensions in our inner cities. In many ways our situation is similar to that which prevailed in the Middle Ages, when, following the Crusades, new knowledge from the Middle East was released; men feared this so much that it gave rise to the suppression of the Templars and the Inquisition. At a time when society is permissive and there can be no return to the Inquisition, it is not surprising that the discipline of our divided denominational structures cannot contain many of the younger generation. This is very much a Glastonbury matter and affects parishes and congregations all over the country. It raises the question as to how far new spiritual energy can be contained within existing structures and whether new forms in addition to house churches and fellowships need to be brought to the birth.

The time has already come when demand for counselling escalates as family life and relationships break down in a multi-

The way forward has to be based on a life of prayer and an adequate spiritual discipline

25

national, multi-cultural, multi-faith society in which relationships between men and women are changing dramatically. People who learn to meditate find nothing like their experience of God in church liturgy and worship. The churches get pushed to the fringe of life and become turned in on themselves. A new world is coming and the churches have to adapt or perish, and the clergy do not know how to meet the situation; we are as people lost in the wilderness.

Nevertheless in Glastonbury there are signs of hope. It is now beginning to be recognized that the churches have a measure of responsibility for those alienated from them and for visitors to Glastonbury. The situation is not easy; no denomination has resources enough to tackle it on its own; old habits die hard but fortunately this question of relating to visitors has been raised at the annual meeting of the local Council of Churches by the Revd Patrick Riley, the new Anglican incumbent.

The Church needs to come out of its buildings and into the community, much of which is not at all respectable

Perhaps it is inevitable that, in an area where Anglicans are much thicker on the ground than other denominations, the lead is likely to be taken in the first place by Anglicans. Glastonbury, however, cannot play an effective role unless all major denominations are involved, and on occasion other denominations both can, and should, provide initiative and leadership. There is a need for the Church to come out of its buildings into the community, the marketplace and the Assembly Rooms, fairs, carnivals, pop festivals — the whole of life, much of which is not at all respectable — if the gulf is to be bridged. On August 6th 1985 a beginning was made by taking a group of individuals on a pilgrimage around Glastonbury with participation of local clergy to explore the spiritual significance of this holy place.

There is a need for a Christian audio-visual to help teach and a Christian counselling centre and meeting point in the heart of the town to supplement what goes on in the Abbey and the churches and the retreat and conference centre. Preferably this would link with local doctors and be for the benefit of all kinds of pilgrims and visitors as well as local residents in need of spiritual help. For this the assistance of religious orders and communities would be invaluable. As we learn to draw on our united Christian inheritance there is need for a community of Christian people who may live in different houses but share a common discipline. Already there are some who are looking in this direction; the heart of the problem is whether the churches will rise to the challenge, or whether new splinter groups will come into being.

During 1985 Rosemary composed music and words for the *Glastonbury Hymn*, now on a record with other hymns and poetry; her music and song based on the objects of the Mothers' Union has been used in Wells Cathedral. Both Rosemary and James have been to Ireland including Newry, Belfast and Armagh, and James, whenever possible with Rosemary, continues visiting Sussex, Hampshire, Dorset, Wiltshire, Devon, Cornwall, St David's in Wales, East Anglia, as well as Somerset and Avon. Much that is good is happening through Healing Guilds and the Acorn Christian Healing Trust; links have been formed with work of reconciliation based on Ammerdown and with religious communities including St Peter's Convent at Woking. As the Spirit of God in Christ Jesus breathes new life into the churches, the people of God are beginning to prepare to move forward.

In conclusion, there is hope that we will meet the challenge and muddle of alternative spirituality by a discipline of prayer with special reference to the Bible and Sacraments. There is a common pool of spirituality within the churches which could help bring people together and give us a sense of purpose and destiny in the life of the Church and nation still largely lacking as 1985 comes to an end. Is it too much to hope that in 1986, the year which should see the launch of the book by Brian Frost about the life and discipleship of the late Marjorie Milne, there will be a further move forward?

A common pool of spirituality within the churches could help give a sense of destiny

The shape of things to come is far from clear but the journey has begun. There is a long way to go, but if there can be a coming together of the whole people of God centred in the true Cross, the British nation may yet wake up one morning to find the Christian Church here is once again a mighty army standing in our midst no longer dead, as God was thought to be in the 1960s, but very much alive and part of the whole universal Church in earth, paradise and heaven.

1986 was the year that Brian Frost published his biography *Glastonbury Journey: Marjorie Milne's search for reconciliation*, about the anchoress who had first introduced James to Glastonbury.

James began sending his annual newsletter in January rather than December, hence there is no letter dated 1986.

January 1987

Thíʀ∂ Glastonbuʀy Newsletter

The prophetic role of Glastonbury

Turmoil

1986 has been a year of political and religious turmoil in which the BBC has again been shown to be more objective than the churches in reporting religious events. Our denominational and party structures and alliances mean that each sees only a part of the truth, is inward-looking, unable after centuries of separation to listen and learn from one another without many people feeling deeply threatened. No wonder structures creak and groan and the churches are seen as out of touch; people like Gerald Priestland and Rosemary Harthill show that our religion and theology have become separated from life. As opposition to the Bishop of Durham bears witness, the way for the Church to return to the centre of life is hard. Many church members prefer the Church to stay where she is; better be safe than involved in conflict, to serve Mammon rather than God, to know the form of religion but not its power.

Nevertheless the Word of God is breaking in; the wind of change blows stronger, revealing that ultimate authority does not lie with the papacy or the Vatican, synods, bishops, the

Church Commissioners, the Methodist Conference, prophets, priests or PCCs, but with God. People cry for peace in a world and nation in turmoil; the churches struggle to communicate spiritual truth but have no credible message even if spiritual "bosses" from many faiths meet together in Assisi; St Francis provides some measure of mutual understanding, perhaps because of his love for natural creation and the poor — which no one can associate with Rome, London, Washington, or Moscow. He proclaimed the Gospel untainted with western European imperialism or misunderstood Greek philosophy.

St Francis' love for creation and the poor: no one can say that of Rome, London, Moscow or Washington

The Church of England, whose clergy are largely trained in terms of Greek philosophy with remains of Latin thinking, fails to communicate with a generation educated in terms of natural science which finds itself deeply divided between left and right, rich and poor. The sins of the industrial revolution come home to roost, exposing our materialism and intellectual pride which has made many turn to atheism, alternative spirituality, or drugs — some respectable, some not — and others to set up Christian fellowships apart from mainstream churches. In all this Glastonbury is no exception. It is part of our history, for that same division was reflected in the wealth and power of the medieval Abbey and the poverty of the people. Nearer the truth in Christ was the Celtic Church and the Saxon Church which in AD987 founded from Glastonbury a community at Cerne Abbas in Dorset, now the home of nearby Anglican Franciscans.

Spirituality through conflict — Marjorie Milne

Inevitably, because Glastonbury has been host to many different spiritual forms from pre-Christian times, it has been and still is a focal point for conflict. Because of this, it holds the key to the emergence of a spirituality which embraces the truth to be found in them all and to expose egocentric satanic power now coming into the open in Britain and worldwide. It is the power which seeks to control political and financial institutions, industrial and energy resources, education, press and television, the armed forces and judiciary, and if possible the Church in every land; defeated by Jesus on the Cross, Satan still attempts to remain prince of this world and would have us serve Mammon not God. This same conflict is written into the hills and buildings and ruins of Glastonbury like a book to read as we seek to learn from Celts and their Indo-European predecessors, from Saxon and Norman, from Hebrew and Jew, from modern immigrants and visitors who come here from many lands in this day and age. Glastonbury insists that spiritual unity and renewal can never come through sectarian beliefs and rules imposed on the whole Church. As St Paul said, Love never fails.

To love God in Christ and through him, to live in God's presence and to know God, is to open up areas of personality and understanding familiar to Celtic–Hebrew Christianity, though to some it is vague, unsatisfactory, ambiguous, not rational or logical. Others, outside of the churches, turn to love from cold-hearted moralism, which is identified by them with churchgoing, and find themselves being accused by churchpeople of being pagan or even satanic. Many of them are humble and open but have little understanding of what is meant by sin, perhaps because churchpeople have put it before them in unacceptable terms.

If we accept that there is much to learn from alternative spirituality, Glastonbury becomes a place which can be a bridge between people who hold deep convictions, which divide conservative from progressive, scientist from artist, papist or republican from royalist. It demands a life of prayer and meditation leading to changed attitudes, inner purification and contemplation. Sadly this is more familiar to some of those involved with the Chalice Well, the Glastonbury Experience and the Assembly Rooms and to the poor than to many in the churches, even if it was pioneered at a deeper and firmly Christian level by Marjorie Milne.

> Glastonbury can bridge between people who hold deep convictions … it demands a life of prayer

Glastonbury Journey

The book *Glastonbury Journey: Marjorie Milne's search for reconciliation* was written by Brian Frost and launched by Bishop Lesslie Newbigin in Glastonbury Town Hall after an ecumenical service of Holy Communion in St John's Church on August 6th. As the book reveals, Christians can reach out to those of alternative spirituality without getting swept away by false christs or the enthusiasm of those who see all light as coming from God, even when it is offbeat and worse. This is timely when Celtic insights, which continued as spiritual undercurrents, are re-emerging, despite St Augustine of Canterbury in AD597, St Wilfrid at the Synod of Whitby in AD667 and "Romanizers" ever since seeking to drive them out of the Church and even exterminate those who held them. Marjorie Milne saw that recovery of neglected Celtic forms of prayer and spirituality related to God and everyday life and work of ordinary people, not far perhaps from primitive Benedictine spirituality, could enable Glastonbury to become a place reborn — the seedbed of a new movement towards unity with those whose insights into truth in Christ differ from ours.

We can reach out to alternative spiritualities without getting swept away by false christs

This means not just acknowledging we have been wrong and asking forgiveness for past accumulation of power and wealth (the hallmark of the Papacy, the Crown, Prince Bishops, religious orders and denominations) but facing deep inner fears which give rise to conflict. Without this there can be no spiritual integrity in the Church to enable us to see off the spiritual challenge of fascism or Leninist communism and the dark occult forces that go with them; we would remain stuck in sectarian attitudes which give rise to schism.

Israelite as well as Christian

The challenge of Marjorie Milne is not just living out changed attitudes to power and wealth; she resigned from the Glastonbury Council of Churches because of the treatment of a British Israelite Christian. She was convinced that European economic and political union, towards which the British people have been manipulated by Parliament, creates a false power block unlike the British Commonwealth which, by integration of rich and poor nations, can prepare the way for the coming to earth of the Kingdom of God. The passion for true freedom associated with Britain at its best also has its roots in a right understanding of Monarchy. It is part of our great cultural heritage which owes its origin to Hebrew, Celtic and Christian-Saxon roots. Britain should be a holy land just as much as the holy land in the Middle East, with Glastonbury the New Jerusalem. Of this role and destiny the Church has lost sight.

If the vision of the writers of the preface to the King James version of the Bible was somewhat nationalistic and had a false concept of kingship, its concept of "Our Zion" comprising England, Wales, Scotland, Ireland and France as a counter to the Hapsburg Empire backed up by the Papacy was relevant at this time, even if it eventually led to the situation with Ian Paisley in Northern Ireland who sees that country as a "holy land" entrusted to Protestants; elsewhere the same Calvinist concept gave rise to the extreme form we now see holding power in South Africa. What can lead to mediation and true freedom for one generation in one nation may be corrupted and lead to slavery and racial conflict with much bloodshed when we forget that Jesus taught that the Lord our God is One Lord, Father of all men, even if God gives nations specific roles in history as he wills.

It is vital, however, to guard not only against nationalism but also against a false universalism centred on a deal between Rome and fascism or communism like that which developed following the 4th-century agreement between the Church and Constantine. Marjorie Milne saw that a true form of the "British Israelite" movement could help Britain recover a sense of community, of destiny and purpose, a right relationship with the land, following the loss of her Empire; in this Glastonbury has a role to play.

Glastonbury has links with Celtic High Kings and Saxon "Bretwalda", reminding us that our Royal Family is connected not only with Saxon, Welsh, Scottish and Irish kings but with Hebrews and Jews of the dispersion. Perhaps their descendants as defenders of the faith can help us recover a spiritual role related to true freedom. Instead of seeking to dominate the world by force of arms — nuclear or conventional — perhaps the Royal Family, by following in the footsteps of

Instead of seeking to dominate the world by force, the Crown can help the poor and deprived

Jesus, can help pave the way for right relationships with the poor and deprived, including immigrants in our inner cities, and for an acceptable role for Rome as a major world Christian centre which would honour the Archbishops of Canterbury and Westminster and leaders of the Free

Jesus has power precisely because he is powerless

Churches. Glastonbury bears witness, as one church leader put it to me, that "There can be no unity without the Royals." Jesus has power precisely because he is powerless; unity comes when power is dispersed and coercion becomes out of date; a basis for leadership emerges which was at the heart of the highest Celtic spiritual tradition of episcopacy and kingship.

Bringing St Dunstan up to date

The 1,000th anniversary of St Dunstan is due to be celebrated in Glastonbury and Baltonsborough, his birthplace nearby, in 1988. Local preparations have already begun. We are presented with an opportunity to break free of the hold which the past has upon us if we face the confusion which existed in the early Church, which stemmed from the decision of the Council of Jerusalem in AD49 to free Gentile Christians for evangelical outreach to the world. This decision led to much confusion and disagreement but it enabled the Church to break free of ingrown Jewish spirituality, until attempts were made to introduce uniform faith and church order in defence of "Christian civilization". In the Middle East and Africa conflict grew up between Christians who were nationalist and those who supported the Roman Empire, paving the way for the rise of Islam. In northern and western Europe Celtic insights were suppressed because of a zeal for freedom, coupled with evangelistic zeal and holiness. There followed under St Dunstan the end of Celtic monasticism in Glastonbury and the establishment of the Benedictine form — and until this day there is scandalous disregard of Pelagius, and the contribution of the Welsh Church, by theologians and historians who also neglect or suppress the historical contribution of the Greek Church including Bishop Aristobulus. In addition St Patrick and St Wilfrid are still regarded as "apostles" of Ireland and Sussex respectively although there were a substantial number of priests active in both areas before they arrived on the scene. Imposed order and renewal may bring short-term benefits but pave the way for long-term destruction, maybe after hundreds of years, as happened in Glastonbury in 1539.

From that time, for 300 years, Glastonbury ceased to have national and international significance but in the 19th century the refounding of religious orders led to renewed interest in holy places. It coincided with the publication of the dogma of the immaculate conception in 1854, papal infallibility in 1870, the bull declaring Anglican Orders invalid in 1896, and the first Roman pilgrimage in Glastonbury in 1894. With the first Anglican pilgrimage in 1897, when several hundred Anglican bishops and archbishops in England for the Lambeth Conference came to Glastonbury, battle lines were being drawn.

> After 300 years, the refounding of religious orders led to renewed interest in holy places

Evangelicals and those who reject priestly domination do not see the importance of holy places, but Romans, High Anglicans, some Freechurchmen, novelists, poets and dramatists, together with astrologers and some spiritists, do; so do those who prefer psychology and magic (white and black) to true spirituality. How much easier to avoid the challenge of discovering what makes for true unity and simply defend former battle lines!

Gradually members of Glastonbury churches are coming to realize that this tangled situation must be faced, and that we need to draw on both "Catholic" and "Celtic" insights so that every section of the One Church can be purified; then we can communicate the Christian faith to those alienated from the churches. It means ensuring that the negative as well as the positive side of St Dunstan, who was indeed a very great Christian, is faced. As a Saxon he was inevitably somewhat prejudiced. Aren't we all? For unity in diversity Christians are still far from ready. Perhaps a recovery of true community depends upon a fuller living relationship with the Trinity, and with natural and supernatural creation and the world of work and everyday life (which Celts knew), and the bridging of the gulf between the Church and the natural sciences. If progress has been made in the area of religion and medicine with the upsurge of the Christian healing ministry, there is a long way to go in the area of natural science, e.g. where the Peace and Green movements are involved. Difficulty comes when one aspect of truth is treated as the whole.

When theology is divided against itself not only are people kept in spiritual infancy but people are destroyed spiritually by vain blasts of doctrine from the Church, whose true task it is to provide in Christ the key to life. In Glastonbury there is an opportunity to seek profound and far-reaching spiritual renewal centred on the person of Christ Jesus, which could pioneer a form of unity with a message of national and international significance. This could lead to resurrection here in Glastonbury; in one sense it has already begun and is now coming into the churches. It cannot but lead to changed male–female understanding and hopefully resolving age-old quarrels about the Blessed Virgin Mary.

Glastonbury could pioneer a unity with international significance

Whatever the Bishop of London and the more conservative elements in the Roman and Orthodox churches — and some hard-line male-dominated Protestants — may think, changes have already started. Those who insist that all Christians must be ultra-conservative and await majority decisions by what purports to be the whole Church must learn not to trample on the rights of others to dissent. There is no warrant in Scripture for it; it is a recipe for schism. It does not mean rejecting the role of the Blessed Virgin as Mother of God, in the light of the incarnation of Jesus and the Cross or in terms of contemplative prayer, if women are ordained to the priesthood; it means accepting Celtic insights even by those whose bones cry out it is wrong, and learning from mixed communities like Pilsdon and Lee Abbey, even if it makes St Dunstan turn in his grave! As a royal priesthood the male people of God in a rapidly changing world can set women free to express their gifts, which may include the power of absolution and to celebrate the Eucharist as ordained people. This is already happening in some of the Free Churches and in parts of the Anglican Communion. To resist this is to cause schism just as much as to advocate female dominance; the real enemy is abuse of power — by both sexes.

Denominational structures

At the Council of Jerusalem in AD49 freedom was won for the Gentile churches to respond to God, to Jesus and the Holy Spirit, provided that practices connected with witchcraft, egocentric powers and seriously debased religion were avoided. We were left to work out how best tribal, national, even individual, insights can be related to what is known to be true in Hebrew–Jewish Law. The 4th-century and later Church of Rome did not like this, and sought the destruction of the Celtic Church which had learnt to relate Christian insights to Hebrew and other insights associated with the Druids. Here lie roots of our denominational differences in Britain and **Rome did not like this diversity and sought the destruction of the Celtic Church. Here lie roots of denominations** Ireland, including Roman, Anglican, Methodist, Baptist, Evangelical forms and Jehovah's Witnesses. People have to begin from where they are, as they start the journey up the mountain towards God. This means that all and sundry cannot honestly share in the sacrament of Holy Communion; all of us draw the line somewhere and it is hypocrisy to pretend there is unity where there is not (as James has found in growing measure this year, especially when relating ecumenically to Roman Catholics); it makes for deep joy when one can share on a true and honest basis as equals before God.

In his desire for unity Jesus was not calling for one great organization which papers over the cracks, but for holiness. Saints and truly contemplative mystics who genuinely love unity find unity with God and each other, which those who live after the flesh cannot. This excludes most members of our churches — even those of the same denomination. If since Vatican II Rome has partly given up its claim to universal oversight of the whole Church (though ARCIC throws some doubt on this [the Anglican–Roman Catholic International Commission, which began annual meetings in 1970]) we are faced with a major problem. How can we begin to find unity with those Christians concerned with astrology and tarot cards, psychic and natural healing, or who relate to Freemasonry or departed spirits? Such share with aspirations of many outside of the churches who are into the "occult", whereas others believe that such practices led to their own spiritual death and that all those who are "reborn of the Spirit" must renounce such practices plus gambling, dancing, alcohol, drugs and whatever they believe leads to hellfire and damnation not just for them but for all. Further, our national group and other loyalties land us in situations where others regard us as being in deep outer darkness, which may or may not be true. Fortunately Christ is there even in outer darkness!

It seems that some form of denominational structures are a necessity; we all need some form of discipline within which to grow; there is need for flexibility, for freedom for people to move around between denominations, being part of a body of people without being judgemental of those on a different route up the mountain to God, and for denominations themselves to be free to change and, if need be, to die so that new forms of alliance can arise. We no longer accept what our ancestors believed without question. And it is in this confused situation that the Church, the precise nature of which is a mystery, has to communicate the faith to those outside and to work out what makes for creative life-giving relationships between bishops, priests and people in the local churches. The claim of fundamentalist evangelical Christianity, which purports to be non-denominational, to be the seat of true unity is false — especially when arguments are used to obtain converts from the "clapped-out" mainstream denominations. Yet paradoxically it is through the challenge of such movements and of Rome that renewal comes to the whole of the Church. On the way it is inevitable that there will be opposition from

It is no use trying to contain the Church within outdated limits — God goes on ahead of us

clergy and ministers whose livelihood depends on attracting support and who feel threatened by renewal if they cannot control it.

Glastonbury Christianity, like that of the British nation, has been finally set towards decline. And if we are to go over to the offensive now that the Empire has disappeared, we have to find forms relevant to the new situation. It is no use trying to contain the Church within limits which have become outdated. God goes on ahead of us as Christ leads us into all truth so that we may have a sense of purpose and attain our true destiny. Hopefully this will give us the spiritual energy which can help bring salvation to our national life just like John Wesley did, without being sectarian or divisive. The 1,000th anniversary of St Dunstan to be celebrated in 1988 provides just the opportunity needed, and it is suggested that the first step is the formation of a body of Christians during 1987, whose members will care for pilgrims and travellers to Glastonbury just like the Hospitallers of an earlier age who owed allegiance to, and yet were often in conflict with, the institutional church.

The Hospitallers

The roots of the Hospitallers lie in ancient tribal hospitality in the Old Testament and in the "undivided" Church of the Middle Ages. To care for people regardless of their origin and status can be to begin to provide renewal for the whole Church without being afraid of tackling both psychic and spiritual truth in Christ. It needs a discipline which is firm, making room for differing interpretations and pastoral practice, balancing love and forgiveness with law and justice. It means accepting those who have broken marriage, ordination and other religious vows and promises in the way Jesus dealt with the woman caught in the act of adultery: he told her to go and sin no more. No one objects to setting up a Christian hospice and it makes sense to have an open door to care for pilgrims and visitors from the kind of four-way centre which Marjorie Milne saw should emerge in Glastonbury. To be effective it has to sort out those in genuine need from spongers.

To care for people regardless of status can begin renewal for the whole Church ... It requires an understanding of paradox

To be involved requires an understanding of paradox common to the Celtic tradition which can help those who have been caught in situations which have involved breakdown (including mental breakdown) and priests, monks and nuns who have left religious orders after life vows and who have run foul of the Church Establishment. It helps pave the way for dissent being accepted by the Church instead of being driven out and accused of schism. It would help pave the way for the return to the Church of those attracted to alternative spirituality and those alienated by moralistic legalism or the denominational squabbles of much of the Christian Church. It does not paper over the cracks but seeks to reconcile persons to God in the light of the Cross and the cosmic Christ,

Not papering over the cracks but reconciling persons to God

through whom is creation and redemption, and draws on Celtic insights with deep awareness of the living, loving presence of God in everyday life. People on this wavelength are to be found both within and outside of Glastonbury and other churches. Thus hospitality like this can give expression to what is already there locally and nationally. If it has not started earlier it is because the time was not yet ripe, partly because of the Greenlands situation. Nevertheless initial steps have already been taken by the churches.

1986 news

Following the injunction granted to Mendip District Council under a High Court order, reluctant steps were taken by the owner, Mrs Alison Collyer, to expel travellers from Greenlands Farm. Steps have also been taken towards the transfer of land and animals to the Paddington Farm Trust but final decisions await the coming of 1987. On one occasion vigilantes have shown they are still active but remain blind to the possible consequences of their actions. Wise decisions never go hand in hand with feeling threatened — even if there are political activists and drug-pushers muscling in on Glastonbury at Greenlands and elsewhere; confrontations beyond the law are counterproductive even if the law of the land is not equal and fair in the sight of God and the weak go to the wall. A growing number of people who have been at Greenlands, some freed from drug dependence, are now working and supporting themselves. With a stronger Christian presence more could have been achieved. At Greenlands there is comparative peace.

Children's World and Gog Theatre, centred on Glastonbury, have made considerable progress even if immature fundamentalist evangelical Christians think they are engaged in witchcraft. This demands great patience and love as response.

Hardliners into black magic are few but those who see demons at Greenlands, the Gothic Image, Glastonbury Experience, and the Chalice Well are like spiritual vigilantes; perhaps the Church can help them grow up? If we learn to handle re-emergence of gnostic and other heresies wisely we will not run foul of poets, artists, musicians, novelists and dramatists who challenge our limitation of God, giving rise to battle lines like those which emerged in Old Testament times between true and false prophets and teachers or in Glastonbury at the beginning of the 20th century. Condemnation of those involved in alternative spirituality as pagans in need of conversion may aggravate rather than heal and unite like Jesus. The Assembly Rooms may yet emerge as a centre for reconciliation and creative art as envisaged by those who built it in the early years of this century and who attracted to Glastonbury a host of people of the calibre of George Bernard Shaw, Laurence Housman, and Fr Gilbert Shaw. The rebirth of a place like Glastonbury is fraught with pitfalls; theological rows in the past have not helped.

The rebirth of Glastonbury is fraught with pitfalls; theological rows in the past have not helped

The appointment of the Revd Peter Hancock as Bath and Wells diocesan healing adviser is a great step forward but it needs to be realized that to be effective and unitive he has to walk a tightrope because of the many different and limited insights held by clergy and laypeople who practise this ministry in all sorts of ways; like medical and surgical practice there is room for different approaches and attitudes to natural and psychic gifts and even spiritism, all of which are to be found within the Church. The rise of bureaucracy and administration means that pastoral and healing work which has been neglected for so long is having to be tackled by someone. God does not leave himself without witness, even if the Church Establishment or those into renewal do not approve. None of us have yet "attained to the fullness of the stature of Christ" nor, in the main, do we have the spiritual discernment to say who is and who is not satanic. Such accusation may be slanderous, libellous, or both. The tongue can be a more dangerous weapon than the sword.

Links continue to be strengthened with religious communities and churches, especially in the southwest and south Wales, and there is a move forward towards the establishment of an above-ground group related to Glastonbury churches in 1987. By the time of the 1,000th anniversary of St Dunstan in 1988 there is hope of progress towards reconciliation on the local scene of Celtic, Saxon, Roman and Orthodox forms of spirituality so that Glastonbury can make a contribution towards reconciliation. We have to remember that there can be no peace in Britain until a solution is found acceptable to the peoples of Ireland and to the two nations, the rich powerful southeast of England and the rest. Here in Glastonbury we stand on the dividing line.

Various developments continue which relate to Glastonbury. There is the new venture at Huntham Cottage, Stoke St Gregory (near where King Alfred burnt his cakes before defeating the Danes), and other places and groups about which it is too early to write; most of all prayer is needed both within and outside of Glastonbury.

St Margaret's Chapel with its concern for those in need of care is a place recognized by the alternative spirituality as being the nearest there is to a chapel of unity, though a new openness at St John the Baptist's Anglican Church is promising. St Patrick's Chapel, where Marjorie Milne prayed for years, is not easily accessible as people have to pay to get into the Abbey grounds; the "poor" and the Alternatives do not see why they should support a divided Church which, with the divided spiritual inheritance from which many suffer through being descended from different denominations in conflict, exposes their need for spiritual integration. The Church as it is gives no effective help and at times aggravates the position. In challenging present structures surely they are right; at rock bottom we all long for a unity which transcends all boundaries. There has been progress in 1986 reflected in this letter but there is a very long way to go. The Pilton pop festival is to be held again in 1987; maybe the day will come when the Church of God takes this seriously and puts the effort into a Christian presence there reflecting that Christians are ready to come out of their ghettoes and get stuck into life.

January 1988

Fourth Glastonbury Newsletter

Seven years after the Turnbulls moved to Glastonbury, 1987 has been a demanding year; there have been many developments both in Glastonbury and in the southwest. Many are receiving what they believe to be a direct call from God to come here; Glastonbury is usually sceptical, and such people often have a difficult apprenticeship. There is a deep and wide gulf between church people and those alienated from the churches, which sticks out like a sore thumb in Glastonbury.

Children's World

1987 began with a crisis situation for Children's World (director Arabella Churchill, granddaughter of Sir Winston). Given notice to quit temporary headquarters in Glastonbury by Christmas 1986, accused of witchcraft and prayed against by hardline evangelical charismatic Christians, opposition was whipped up and barred purchase of premises in Ashcott, five miles from Glastonbury. During this period James, who respected what Children's World was seeking to do, was invited to become and became a trustee of this registered charity. God took a hand and excellent premises were purchased near the centre of Glastonbury at a low price because squatters had moved in. They moved out once they knew that Children's

World was involved. It is lust for money that such people oppose, not those who have a genuine concern for people. Children's World, some six years after its foundation, is now valued not only by schools — especially those concerned with handicapped children — but by commercial and educational "establishments" around, and even by some in the churches. It raises the question why imaginative ventures like Children's World, which help unemployed young people gain a sense of worth, who work for low rates of pay *and* mediate abundant life to isolated insecure, unhappy children in our schools, come under such vicious attack from well-to-do "Christians" who condemn and make no attempt to relate personally to those involved.

Why do imaginative ventures come under such vicious attack from well-to-do 'Christians'?

Greenlands Farm

After a second High Court action, Greenlands Farm has at last passed out of the possession of Mrs Alison Collyer and into the hands of the Paddington Farm Trust, a registered charity started, partly by Paddington churches, to help children and families in the inner cities recover their rural roots. The Turnbulls moved to Glastonbury in 1980 partly because they knew major difficulties lay ahead which could undermine the vision of Marjorie Milne (and visions and dreams of others) of Glastonbury as a focal point for reconciliation. So this solution at Greenlands, though far from perfect, is perhaps better than moving from crisis to crisis until the strain causes final collapse.

Whilst there is still much about the changeover better left unsaid, it is well to record that many young people, some mentally sick, owe their chance in life to Mrs Collyer, who provided that chance at considerable personal cost. If her open-door policy did attract a small disruptive element related to the "Peace Convoy", it helped many deprived and homeless people as well as women and children, at a time when government policy caused riot police to take drastic action at Molesworth and Stonehenge, whence came many refugees to Greenlands Farm. If one may disagree with Mrs Collyer over some of her actions (and James has certainly done this) both the Turnbulls

44

would agree that for sheer guts, determination and persistence in helping people who suffer, this OAP has few equals. Hopefully Greenlands Farm will eventually be seen as having played a crucial role in helping Glastonbury break free of our self-centred factional quarrels and defensiveness against the poor and dispossessed, coupled with lack of vision, which are roots of decline. Greenlands raises the question "Where is the Church when it comes to tackling the burning issues of the day?" The answer would seem to be "Engaged in doctrinal wrangles, maintenance of structures, and superficial gestures of unity in worship." Old Testament prophets would no doubt denounce a church in which the Abbey makes no provision for the poor and forgets that rules which serve the interests of the well-to-do will always be opposed; even the annual Anglican and Roman pilgrimages have scarcely begun to tackle the roots of religious suspicion and distrust which are as deep as those which divide President Reagan from Mr Gorbachov. We all tend to make God in our own image and hold to any substitute for the one God who is both beyond and in the midst.

> And where is the Church? Doctrinal wrangles, maintenance of structures and superficial gestures of unity in worship

Religious orders and Glastonbury

The Greenlands Farm venture had its origin when a number of young people, including Jim Nagel, now a sub-editor of the *Central Somerset Gazette*, who related to Marjorie Milne of 21 Manor House Road (near where Mrs Collyer now lives in a council flat) got hold of a green bus and proceeded to tour religious orders and communities — Roman, Anglican, ecumenical and Free Church — to tell abbots and other leaders both male and female that their orders needed a shake-up.

They were joined by Mrs Anna Harper from Sussex Square, Brighton. She, with Brother Mark SSF, had first met us in 1966 at Sayers Common, Sussex, where James was vicar. She hoped to find premises in Brighton for young people hooked on heroin; as funds were not forthcoming she opened her doors to up to 30 young people, some of whose friends had already died.

Anna loved people, accepting them as they are, and eventually landed herself in financial disaster. James introduced her to Marjorie Milne, who also came to Sayers Common in 1966 after she had read articles he had written about God, the Church, Christian unity, farming, and the land. Behind this lay wartime experience in many countries, years in industry and commerce related to world trade and agriculture, and theological training under the direction of Bishop George Bell, Canon (later Bishop) Kenneth Sansbury and Bishop Noel Hall of India.

Various steps which also began in 1966 led to the establishment of a major Roman Catholic ecumenical centre in Sayers Common, where Rosemary and James led a day, part of a weekend in Sussex, in July 1987, to share insights gained from living in Glastonbury. Over the years the Turnbulls had been brought into contact with Lee Abbey, Crowhurst, Green Pastures, The Guild of Health, Post Green, Whatcombe House, the Churches' Council for Health and Healing, the Anglican Benedictines at Nashdom, and the SSF at Hilfield Friary in Dorset. Many people we met knew Marjorie Milne, including Brian Frost and others; contact came with Pilsdon, Ammerdown, Buckfast Abbey and Downside Abbey.

What drew James to Marjorie was her belief — which he shared — that the world faces a crisis of cosmic proportions involving natural creation which a largely urbanized church does not understand. When "God was dead" in the 1960s young people starved of meditation and contemplation took to drugs and Eastern religion and began to rediscover the importance of Mother Earth; rejecting Western materialism they sought to share in the poverty of the Third World which the West had exploited, unaware of impending ruin. Marjorie Milne made James aware that Glastonbury could not become a focal point for renewal and reconciliation without the participation of religious orders and communities of every kind so that the many differing strands that relate here can be reconciled, each strand free to pursue the course right for those

46

who belong to it but related to the whole. The Abbey cannot just be Benedictine (Anglican or Roman), for Glastonbury of its nature is home to both left and right in politics, including extremes, to pagan religion as well as to Christian insights shared with Free Church as well as Anglican, Roman and Orthodox Christians — that is its glory and its challenge.

> Glastonbury's glory and challenge is that it is home to both left and right, pagan as well as Christian

The Assembly Rooms

God may have seemed to be dead in the 1960s but awareness of Glastonbury as a major world spiritual centre moving towards rebirth was spreading. Amsterdam may have become a centre for the distribution of drugs but Holland like Glastonbury became a centre for new-age thinking involving people deep into astrology and other faiths. Some hold that it is all of fascist inspiration with roots not in heaven above but rising from areas of creation below, of which our more ignorant rationalists do not seem to be aware. From Holland in the late 1970s came Willem and Helene Koppejan with British Israelite contacts including Isabel Hill Elder, an author who researched deeply into Celtic and Hebrew spirituality and history. They founded the Glastonbury Experience and, soon after, Willem died, leaving his wife Helene to carry on. She linked up with Geoffrey Ashe, scholar and author, who has written several books on the Arthurian legends-cum-history and who saw the rebirth of Glastonbury as on the way.

They and others realized that the Assembly Rooms with its past history as a centre for community arts could help Glastonbury fulfil a new role under conditions very different from the 1920s and 1930s, when Britain was very insular and the movement of the Spirit towards unity and healing had scarcely begun. A small body of trustees was formed and in 1977 the Assembly Rooms, then in a very dilapidated state, was rented from Somerset county council at a nominal rent on the understanding that some repairs were carried out. Part of the premises were let to Gog Theatre Ltd, a registered charity founded by Tom Clark, a member of the Street family whose predecessor Roger had played a major role more than fifty years before. Gog has become one of the leading touring drama groups in the southwest involved in education.

Gradually a growing number of young people, including homeless and unemployed people, social misfits and Greenlanders, and others who found the churches had nothing to offer, sought an alternative spirituality based on the Assembly Rooms. They began to catch a vision of what could be and some of them started work voluntarily to repair the building and to use the poor facilities which were all that could be provided. James got drawn in because of his involvement with Greenlands and when the "Friends of the Assembly Rooms" was founded in 1985 he started to give some measure of backing to the young people who were there, and after a time became a member of the Friends. This was a change of direction for the Rooms, which began to provide care for the poor including travellers — which the Abbey and the Church were not doing.

Sections of the "respectable" Establishment, including local businessmen, farmers and some church people, felt threatened, and those who feared the "occult" were condemnatory and made no attempt to relate or understand, but support began to grow. For example the Revd Patrick Riley, the new Anglican vicar, became to some extent involved in so far as other commitments allowed. Before the tenancy arrangement with the county council expired in 1987 a new trust was formed to endeavour to purchase the Assembly Rooms with encouragement and help from the former trustees and from county councillors and county staff with wide experience of social questions. James was elected a trustee and became treasurer.

'Respectable' sections and those who feared the 'occult' made no attempt to relate or understand

In spite of criticism (some of which was and still is justified), December 1987 saw a celebration party after the purchase had been completed, at which Edith Rice (four times mayor and one of the former trustees for some years), Geoffrey Ashe, Michael Keery (the present mayor), and Mrs Jean Pike (a former councillor and member of the new trustee body) spoke.

Hopefully this will help dispel some of the doubts about what goes on in the Assembly Rooms. There is still a long way to go but with £11,000 raised in three months, and the hope of a community worker for Glastonbury (where one is badly needed) in 1988, the venture is now off the ground. Although many difficulties and challenges still have to be faced, the prophets of gloom who abound in Glastonbury have so far been confounded.

The need for more prayer

During his six years relating to Greenlands Farm, which came to an end following the first High Court action and the departure of the "peace convoy" in 1987, there had been some sort of weekly "prayer meeting" held on the farm. James had not undertaken a single-handed apostolic ministry of deliverance in the name and power of Christ without believing that this work demands a degree of corporate prayer and support from local church members — which was not forthcoming. There had not been either the quality of prayer or in-depth teaching about the healing ministry in the churches and there was not an adequate base at the farm. It is of no value to cast out one devil only to let in seven (to use language from the New Testament, which psychiatrists know about even if they do not use the same words). Now the open door at Greenlands is shut and the front line is in the centre of Glastonbury. The Assembly Rooms, the Abbey, the churches, the Glastonbury Experience, the Gothic Image and the Abbey House are all part of the battle for the soul which is going on.

Opportunities for pastoral work in depth have begun to come. One such came when a woman deep into the occult, black magic and drugs was hacked to death whilst living with an unfortunate young man who was also addicted to drugs and is now in prison. Recently a semi-Christian former Hare Krishna leader was also put to death. A man, who spent the night previous to this incident at Greenlands Farm (the last night before Mrs Collyer left and the open door was finally shut on

An apostolic ministry of deliverance demands prayer and support from local church members

Friday November 13th), indicated that this was what he intended to do. This is of course still *sub judice*.

These examples and others less extreme are indications of the depth to which part of the Church has to go before there is any prospect of the Church commanding the respect of those who see all religions as equal, the cosmic Christ working in all faiths, and the Church as irrelevant to their situation. How do we express spiritual integrity and authentic Christian faith so that people may know that Jesus has overcome death and all the horrors of the world in which we are living, and is King of Kings and Lord of Lords? More and more groups for prayer and study which are outward-looking, together with effective sacraments, are needed if the way is to be found through the jungle of conflicting energies and forces. This means a fully Trinitarian faith so that suffering service and the resurrection power of the Gospel go hand in hand. The message that Glastonbury has for the sleeping beauty of the Christian Church in Britain (like the sleeping beauty in the pantomime story) is that awakening will come only when we cease being afraid of the occult and learn to discern the pointers to truth in magic, natural science and astrology and grapple with the dark forces at work in ourselves and only then go out to overcome in the power of the Holy Spirit.

> Glastonbury's message for the sleeping Church is that awakening will come when we discern pointers to truth in magic, science and astrology

The Turnbulls and the churches

It should be evident that James could not relate to those outside of the churches as well as to those inside without prayer support from friends and an immense amount of help and encouragement from Rosemary, who continues to compose words and music for hymns (some related to Christian healing) and prayers as well as being involved with St Benedict's Church, ecumenical prayer groups, the Deanery Synod, and the Mothers' Union, of which she is becoming deanery presiding member. Having given up piano-teaching, she is now freer to move around on James's visits to Sussex (occasional chaplaincy duty at Crowhurst, Sayers Common etc.), Hertfordshire (Acorn conferences) and various centres in Somerset, Avon, Devon, Dorset, Cornwall and south Wales.

James continues to be involved with the council of the Guild of Health in London. In the southwest, where May Valentine (another friend of Marjorie Milne) has been a tower of strength, opportunities have arisen not only through the Guild of Health but also through Bath and Wells diocesan healing group and the Acorn Christian Healing Trust. This last has involved sharing ministry on occasion with the Revd Peter Hancock, first diocesan healing adviser in Britain. Nationally the Guild of Health is becoming freer to fulfil a shared vision for the future independently of the Marylebone Parish Church setup but relating to it. Again the quality of prayer is crucial; through long association with prayer groups the Guild is in a good position to help develop this ministry and help undergird parish and congregational life. It is complementary to the Churches' Fellowship for Psychical and Spiritual Studies, which, when functioning on a sound spiritual basis, is well placed to help people face traumas and encounters with both natural and spiritual forces.

With the departure of the Revd Michael Hand, curate to the Abbey Five parishes, and pending the arrival of the Revd Stafford Low, James has had extra work to do locally Anglican-wise, but this will be reduced by the end of January and by the end of June still more when Revd Josephine Bax, author of *The Good Wine*, arrives as a woman deacon to augment the paid staff of the Abbey Five. Perhaps this will give James more time to pray and to work for the building up the Kingdom of God, **If it brings conflict with those who hold hardline one-sided theological positions, so be it** ecumenically based on that mediating strain of Christianity which has its root in the ministry of Jesus and of James the "brother of the Lord". If that brings conflict with those who hold hardline one-sided theological positions, whose adherents try to control people, so be it.

Reference must be made to changes at the Abbey House following the departure of the nuns, who have been redeployed. (The Roman nuns departed from the St Louis Convent School some time ago.) Martin Oliver, who came from Leicestershire, is giving the Abbey House a much-needed new look, but the crucial question we now face is whether there can be a real coming together in Glastonbury or whether old tendencies to faction will continue both in the churches and outside. The stubborn self-righteousness of parties in the C of E, which should be both Catholic and Reformed, suggests that some Anglican bishops and more clergy and laity do not understand what mediation is about. The days of Empire and Christian superiority have gone; the C of E "Establishment" in its present form may be going. Christ Jesus is alive and at work outside as well as inside of the churches; no church, not even the Roman or the Orthodox Church, has a monopoly of God. This was made abundantly clear when Rosemary and James were invited by Lord Hylton, who shares many of our concerns, to attend a national prayer breakfast sponsored by members of both houses of Parliament. After breakfast chaired by the Speaker of the House of Commons, members of all political parties and denominations declared that their Christian convictions came before their political allegiance; out of this comes united Christian witness which has a cutting edge in our inner cities and it suggests we are getting nearer that spiritual reawakening this country needs before it is too late.

Church unity in Glastonbury

After several years, with much encouragement from Mary Miller (another friend of Marjorie Milne), chairperson of Glastonbury Council of Churches for three vital years, Rosemary had helped initiate an ecumenical prayer group which visits each church in Glastonbury in turn. During 1987 she and James were invited to plan an ecumenical service in the chancel of the Abbey on Whitsunday. The evangelical Calvinist Gospel Hall and the Cypriot Orthodox Church would not cooperate, nor would the Glastonbury Christian Fellowship, now calling itself the Mid-Somerset Community Church. The belief of such groups that Rome is still in the grip of Satan (which is still true in part, as the death of John Paul I bears witness) and that the middle-of-the-road churches are wishy-washy and also in the grip of Satan makes for difficulty for those who seek genuine ecumenical cooperation.

It is not yet time to give details of all that happened or about Roman Catholic and Free Church contacts both before and after what proved to be a most fruitful occasion. The participants included members of the sacred dance group, who took a prominent part at the farewell to pilgrims which took place in Wells Cathedral to mark the departure of the bishop of Bath and Wells. Whitsunday revealed that there are still elements in the Roman Church that desire the whole of the Church in this country to return to the Roman obedience and that there are Anglican elements determined that the Anglican Church retains control over the Abbey and that there can be no question of sharing control even with the Free Churches. When one considers the historical situation which gave rise to the present trusteeship, it stands out a mile that there is a long hard haul ahead before distrust and suspicion can be overcome and the power game given up; then Christ might be able to return and we Christians give up crucifying him in each other. A disunited church has no answer for Children's World, for Greenlands Farm, for the Glastonbury Experience, for the Assembly Rooms or for the Society of Friends; the local churches cannot attain this degree of unity without help from outside, and it is of no use papering over the cracks.

There is a long hard haul before distrust and suspicion and the power game can be given up

1987 saw the Grail Trust, started by the Revd Jonathan Robinson as director and trustee, also a friend of Marjorie Milne, now vicar of Stoke St Gregory, becoming involved in Glastonbury. Of this trust James became a trustee and treasurer some years ago, joining with the Revd John Pritchard, now vicar of Wilton and formerly diocesan youth officer. The trust made a grant to help finance the purchase of the Assembly Rooms and hopefully will become more involved in 1988 in a form of Christian cooperation acceptable to those outside the churches.

Towards the end of 1987 the Abbey trustees launched an Anglican appeal for £600,000 to finance a major entrance and information complex. Dick Ripper of Promote Avalon Development came up with a project for a major Arthurian exhibition to be centred on that part of Glastonbury, including the Assembly Rooms and the Glastonbury Experience, which housed the medieval monastic school. Martin Godfrey, a local architect and businessman, seeks to link up the civil authority, the Chamber of Commerce, the Abbey, the Assembly Rooms and the Arthurian exhibition.

1988 will see whether Glastonbury will rise to the possibility of a greater unity leading to rebirth, or whether suspicion, distrust, fear and the desire to control take over as each group seeks to keep its own little empire, resulting in more conflict. This newsletter is written in the conviction that there can be no solution without Anglicans and Romans taking the Celtic dimension into account; here lie hidden roots of the two-nations syndrome in Britain. If the lust for power expressed at the Synod of Whitby and still more after the Norman conquest is given up, then there is some hope that the Irish troubles will be nearer solution. It is perhaps significant that 1988 is the 1,000th anniversary of the death of St Dunstan, a controversial figure who sought unity between Anglo-Saxon and Celt — provided it fitted in with his concept of God's will.

Anglicans and Romans must take the Celtic into account; here lie hidden roots of Britain's two-nations syndrome

Finally 1987 saw the conception if not the birth of the Hospitallers of Glastonbury, including Sheena Rees, the social worker who took Marjorie Milne into her home when she had become too ill to manage at Manor House Road, and Jim Nagel and his wife Viola. Hopefully this will move forward in 1988 to provide one ecumenical disciplined Christian base to help meet the challenge of Glastonbury, to seek to bring the disparate functions together, to reach out to those alienated from the churches, and to make provision for the poor and under-privileged which the Abbey and the churches have not done.

January 1989

Fifth Glastonbury Newsletter

Spiritual warfare

Parochial ministry for more than twenty years in Sussex revealed that centres of conflict can become focal points for reconciliation and healing, not expanding at the expense of other parishes or congregations but as bases for praying and caring "communities" concerned with the whole Church, not just with denominational structures which are competitive. This proved good preparation for Glastonbury. Here 1988 brought to the surface more roots of conflicts which have plagued Glastonbury for centuries leading to decline of civil influence, decline of commercial prosperity, poor town planning, poor shopping and social facilities, inadequate access to carparks, disruption of the town centre by heavy traffic, threatened loss of the police station, and decline of the churches. As awareness of the plight of the town grows, the need for change is increasingly recognized, but conflicting interests make for confusion. Travellers and those who some call "weirdos" — attracted by TV programmes about past glories, present oddities and future potential — add to that confusion. Only profound spiritual renewal will enable Glastonbury to break free from the power of self-centred fears and hatreds related to past curses and current destructive arguments which divide the town, which seems to be looking continually for scapegoats to blame for our dilemma. Not surprisingly, Glastonbury is seen by some, including [one senior bishop], as a "queer" place.

To insist that roots of division must be faced in love and charity brings skeletons out of the cupboard, including the need for forgiveness for the judicial murder of Abbot Whiting and his two monks on the Tor and for the Inquisition and events which gave rise to the Reformation and its excesses.

Repentance and forgiveness is essential if Glastonbury is to become a world focus for spiritual renewal

There can be no peace whilst "Christians" still regard each other as satanic and have only surface relationship with each other, as if demonic powers from the past no longer have power. Let there be no doubt that repentance and forgiveness is essential at that level, if Glastonbury is once again to become a major local, national and world focal point for spiritual renewal. Satan must first be defeated at that depth. To believe anything else is illusion; it is to say "peace, peace" where there is no peace. During 1988 battle lines have become clearer: denominational power games have to be given up so that we can face the insecurity, fear and hostility within ourselves which has roots deep in history; all denominations, not only Romans and Anglicans, will find this tough.

History comes alive

During 1988 Glastonbury celebrated major events in both local and national history. These include the 300th anniversary of the "glorious bloodless revolution" of 1688, the 400th anniversary of the defeat of the Spanish Armada, and the 1,000th anniversary of the death of St Dunstan, son of a Saxon noble born at Baltonsborough, the abbot, archbishop and kingmaker, who brought some measure of peace between Saxon and Celt. These events, together with the 250th anniversary of the conversion of John and Charles Wesley, raise questions about principalities and powers, about our role and destiny as a "Christian" nation used time and again — in spite of our pride and failings — to humble dictators bent on European if not world domination. Early in the year, soon after his arrival in Bath and Wells diocese, Bishop George Carey reminded the diocesan advisory group concerned with Christian healing of the need to think — and pray — through such events theologically. First therefore we consider St Dunstan.

St Dunstan's millennium

Dunstan preferred Roman order and spirituality to Celtic and insisted on the right of the Church to control the King and affairs of state. Firmly "orthodox" Christians who reject the power game prefer Alfred the Great, who 100 years before Dunstan took refuge in Athelney near Glastonbury when defeated by the Danes. He learnt much from Welsh and Cornish Christians (not just the Irish as may be falsely believed) and became the "Moses" of Anglo-Saxon Wessex. This reminds us that the Welsh and Cornish kept the flame of civilization alive when Charlemagne and others overran and tyrannized much of western Europe. Why is their contribution still not honoured in England?

St Dunstan introduced Benedictine in place of Celtic spirituality to Glastonbury and in AD973 crowned Edgar as the first King of all England at Bath using a rite similar to that used in AD800 by the then Bishop of Rome for the consecration and enthronement of Charlemagne as "Holy" Roman Emperor. This was after the Merovingian kings of southern "France" with their Hebrew–Celtic connections were overthrown. In Britain we have used this combination of Hebrew and Roman rite for kings (and Roman emperors) ever since.

Edgar the West Saxon was buried in Glastonbury, and shortly before the dissolution of the Abbey in 1540 a chapel was built to his memory sited east of the high altar equidistant to the tomb of Celtic King Arthur. Here in the ruins of the Abbey are pointers to the power struggles which have rent western Europe for more than 1,000 years. Jesus may have insisted that "my kingdom is not of this world", but in Glastonbury earthly kingdoms, politics, and religion are

Here in the ruins of the Abbey are pointers to the power struggles that have rent Europe for a thousand years inseparably intertwined. A truly Christian spirituality which has Glastonbury as a focal point must take this into account as well as a right relationship between religion,

A truly Christian spirituality needs right relationship between religion, science, the cosmic Christ and nature

natural science, the cosmic Christ, and natural creation. The ruins of Glastonbury firmly state that the divine right of Kings and the infallibility of Popes is out; God shares his glory with no other, be they church leader, constitutional monarch, parliamentarian, or dictator. The way to the Kingdom of God lies through the Cross and that alone is our denominational meeting point.

Prophets of the Kingdom

One of the outcomes of the fourth Turnbull newsletter was a request from the Bishop of Chichester for James to visit the Servants of the Will of God at Crawley Down in Sussex. Not only did this mean meeting Brother Mark SSF, friend of Brighton days in the 1960s, but renewing the awareness of the major prophetic role of Gilbert Shaw — whose biography by R. D. Hacking had recently been published — who pioneered an understanding of the Kingdom of God and of Love and community based mainly on the "Great Tradition" of Greek and Latin theology. He helped to inspire not only the Servants of the Will of God but the Sisters of the Love of God at Fairacres, Oxford, who also have a concern for Glastonbury. In this Fr Shaw, spiritual director, exorcist and prophet, goes beyond John Keble, whose sermon on national apostasy in 1833 helped pave the way for the Oxford Movement and heralded a new relationship between C of E, Roman Catholicism, Britain, and Europe. His view of God was primarily transcendent and authoritarian although he was aware of the importance of hours of daily prayer in the "cell" as well as living and worshipping as part of a community, as did the Celts 1500 years ago. He was perhaps preparing for a time when the power of secular institutions such as the Monarchy, Parliament, the armed forces, the police and the judiciary would be shaken before the Kingdom of God fully comes.

On another front James, who prior to ordination had come

into contact with Christian healing through Rosemary's family connections, met the late Fr Jim Wilson of the Guild of Health. Fr Jim's insights into spirituality were linked more with the immanence of God than were Fr Gilbert's. He emphasized natural science, natural creation, daily life and work in the world; his concern for proclaiming the Kingdom of God and healing the sick was also based on medical science which brings in the psychic dimension. The Guild approach, which stems from this but insists on a "clean" spirituality, is concerned with prayer groups, community and the poor; it owes much to St Francis and Mother Julian, it is less authoritarian and more inclusive than the "Great Tradition". Both approaches value contemplative prayer. Together they reconcile opposites and make for a fuller Trinitarian understanding, as found in the Celtic Church.

The Kingdom of God is coming

Glastonbury, which has much to learn from Taizé and Iona, requires a Church based on community free of the lust for power and wealth which has corrupted Western civilization. Perhaps those who left the Lady Chapel on the site of the original Celtic Church and the chapel dedicated to Thomas à Becket standing, when the rest of the Abbey was pillaged, had a concern for the poor we would do well to heed. Today it is not so much the churches but the Alternatives who insist that we must give up the struggle for power which gives rise to institutional and revolutionary violence in South Africa, Northern Ireland, the Soviet Union and many other lands, and of which there are also seeds in Britain. There is a developing world consciousness, referred to in the spring 1988 issue of the magazine *Community*, published by the National Association of Christian Communities and Networks, which gives hope of a Christian spirituality which will help save the world from the darkness and despair which threatens as we approach the 21st century.

> Glastonbury has much to learn from Taizé and Iona: a Church free of the lust for power and wealth

In April 1988 the Revd Dr Martin Israel led three sessions

in Glastonbury Town Hall which were well received by both churchpeople and Alternatives. Whilst these were primarily related to Christian healing there are wider implications for the coming of the Kingdom of God. The roles of St Dunstan and King Alfred in history raise profound questions for us now. How ready is the Church to think and pray through such questions as every part of our foundations are shaken to their roots?

Glastonbury Abbey — 1988

As yet there is no change likely in so far as control of the Abbey is concerned, even if both the Archbishop of Canterbury and the Papal Nuncio came to lead the Anglican and Roman pilgrimages on successive days in June 1988. They followed Douglas Dale, the author who preached on the importance of St Dunstan as a great ecclesiastical politician and spiritual leader at a service of celebration for the 1,000th anniversary of St Dunstan's death on May 17th. This was a reversal of earlier judgement, more in tune with Celtic, Orthodox and anti-Roman tradition, which was harsher on St Dunstan!

On May 22nd, Whitsunday, an ecumenical service in the Abbey under Methodist auspices celebrated the 250th anniversary of the conversion of John and Charles Wesley. James was privileged to be invited to lead prayers for Glastonbury and was able to include prayers for forgiveness for past curses by Christians who excommunicated, tortured and killed one another in the name of God. A price has still to be paid for past separation from our Hebrew roots in Abraham, Isaac and Jacob, and involvement with the nationalism of Moses and even more of Ezra. Perhaps Arthur Koestler was right in stating that the Jews are the mirror in which the rest of the nations will in the end see our own aggressive nationalism. Maybe in Britain in 1988, if not in Ireland, we have forgotten the power of "history", myth, signs, symbols and legends to transform people's attitudes for good or evil. When this happens, religion becomes separated from life, leading to decline in the effective power of the sacraments, decline in the

We forget the power of history, myth, legends, signs and symbols to transform people's attitudes for good or evil

Anglo-Catholic wing of the C of E, in Roman Catholicism as well as in the Free Churches, and a new respect for Orthodoxy, to which the Archbishop of Canterbury referred when reporting on his visit to the Soviet Union on the 1,000th anniversary of the introduction of Christianity to the Ukraine. There, after seventy years of persecution, the monastic and contemplative life is re-emerging purified and renewed. Hardline fundamentalist evangelical Protestants do not have all the answers for this situation, as the Alternatives are not slow to point out. Perhaps Glastonbury can reveal a better way for the Church of God to grow. In this the role of the Abbey could be crucial.

Avalon Library

A major move forward by the Alternatives in 1988 has been the foundation of the Avalon Library, for which a major appeal will be launched in 1989. It is intended to be a world resource centre for study of myth, legend, and spirituality. As with the Assembly Rooms, Geoffrey Ashe (a Roman Catholic with Jewish antecedents), is a key figure. James became a founder member after attending a "symposium", which consisted of a debate between Geoffrey Ashe and Kathy Jones, who writes and produces plays of a very powerful nature which are performed in the Assembly Rooms (Ariadne Productions). The symposium linked the Arthurian legends — about which Geoffrey Ashe is a, if not the, leading world expert — with the effective power of myth, legend and "history" to transform personality, as experienced by Kathy Jones and performers from a wide range of social and cultural backgrounds.

There followed a searching open debate on the role of Christ, whom nearly all present — few were church worshippers — see as crucial, not only for Glastonbury. It revealed that the neglect of the Church in Britain to appeal to the imagination, the heart with its affections, intuition and basic instincts is a major factor in the decline, if not apostasy, from church institutions. Those

> Neglect to appeal to imagination, the heart with its affections, intuition and instincts is a major factor in the decline of the Church

involved in the Avalon Library are in the main aware of their inadequate spiritual resources but are determined not to become subject to a "Christian" Church which regards them as immoral and in need of forgiveness. The truth is that now, as in the days when Jesus walked in human flesh in the Holy Land, there are many who have been sick or sinners who have more experience of forgiveness than many in the churches. The last people to whom many such turn for help are the clergy.

The last people to whom many turn for help are the clergy

Assembly Rooms

Following purchase of the Assembly Rooms in December 1987 by trustees acting on behalf of the "Friends", attempts have been made to bring some measure of order and sound administration into the one place in Glastonbury where the unemployed, travellers, mentally sick and disturbed people, and others who see themselves treated as scapegoats by society, are accepted. Some may be promiscuous, others are into drugs or black magic, run into debt or fall foul of the law. Some are advocates of anarchy; some are of the left, others of the right politically; they are of many religious faiths or none. Without some sense of direction the Assembly Rooms could become like George Orwell's Animal Farm.

Fortunately both the county community-education authority and the Grail Trust are aware of the importance of the Assembly Rooms; grants from both bodies made it possible to appoint a full-time community initiatives officer in November 1988 who will supervise various employment schemes to train unemployed people by means of building projects, plays, the annual dance festival, and care for people who are homeless or deprived. The Assembly Rooms demands numerous meetings to deal with constant crises and personality problems inseparable from such a venture, which includes a recording studio as well as a theatre. Like the Avalon Library it will require substantial funding in 1989. During 1988 the café, which is at the heart of the whole activity, went from crisis to crisis but has survived.

In July a meeting was held in the Assembly Rooms under the auspices of the Grail Trust at which the Revd Stuart Affleck, warden of the Pilsdon community, spoke; there were representatives from the civil authority, including the mayor, town and district councillors, social workers, the churches, and those willing to tackle the problem of homelessness. This proved an acceptable Christian presence and hopefully will help prepare the way for the release of those who have become slaves to dark occult forces both natural and spiritual. One consequence was that in December an approach was made for the involvement of Church Action for the unemployed, which will be followed up in 1989.

Moving forward

Some years ago it seemed to James that the way for Glastonbury to attain its destined role for the coming of the Kingdom of God through increasing world chaos — which some (not for the first time in history) call the "tribulation" — lay with moves forward on two fronts which should eventually link up. The first of these was required in the heart of the churches, the second on the fringes, both backed up by community including the "Hospitallers". The first area demanded improvement in the quality of prayer life leading to a sense of security in God and more openness to people where they are: this means spiritual renewal in the churches. The second area required social action with prayer backing; social work is ineffective unless people are changed and become less self-centred and more God-centred. In different ways Fr Gilbert Shaw and Fr Jim Wilson, Fairacres and Crawley Down, the Guild of Health and charismatic renewal, have pioneered the way forward. SCK [Servants of Christ the King] fellowships of meditation and contemplation, and Julian groups as well as religious orders and communities founded in the 19th and during this century, traditional and new, are on this wavelength.

Social work is ineffective unless people are changed and become less self-centred and more God-centred

For all its faults the Anglican Church in this area is better placed than other denominations to fulfil this role in spite of decline; comprehensiveness is a strength as well as a weakness; in the end in Britain mediation will prevail. Progress is slow and there is some progress in all denominations, but most progress is to be found amongst Anglicans. There will be little place in this deeper renewal for those satisfied with superficial liturgical or free worship, who desire a "holy huddle" or the spirituality of a football-match crowd. Lead will come from committed Christians whose prayer, Biblical awareness and sacramental life enables them to be still in the midst of turmoil and are not afraid. To this the Archbishop of Canterbury's New Year television message bears witness. Around will be false spirituality, illusion and chaos of belief. Glastonbury will be Glastonbury! Fundamentalist holier-than-thou Christians and those who put denominational loyalty first, in spite of the Nicene Creed, and who do not accept those who differ from them as Jesus did, rule themselves out.

Assisi, Glastonbury, and the Kingdom of God

St Francis of Assisi in the 13th century faced a somewhat similar position prior to the Black Death. In 1988 the Turnbulls, who were celebrating their ruby wedding anniversary, were privileged to return to Italy for the first time for forty years and visited Assisi. Following recommendations from a friend, Rosemary and James stayed at the Cittadella Ospitalita inside the walls of Assisi, where they received much help from a Roman Catholic priest who helped them to draw on the deeper wells of the prophetic Franciscan tradition with its concerns for stillness and contemplative prayer, for natural creation, daily work and the poor. So much of this has roots in Hebrew–Celtic spirituality; St Francis's mother came from Provence in the south of France, so this gave him contact, partly through minstrels and troubadours, with St Martin of Tours and the Arthurian legends. There is much in common between Assisi and Glastonbury. Assisi with its "brothers minor" rather than "fathers major" can help us break free of the shackles of the past and carve out a spirituality for a church devoid of power and privilege, against which the gates of hell cannot prevail. Slowly perhaps the way is being prepared with the emergence of a new consciousness (not just for "Hospitallers") to link up the churches and the Alternatives, but the Franciscans and Benedictines, who have a role to play in any eventual Glastonbury renewal.

The future of Glastonbury is inseparable from the role of monarch and state, both under the authority of Christ, as intended by King Alfred the Great; in Christ alone the lion lays down with the lamb as prophesied by Isaiah, as we should be reminded when we look at the Royal Coat of Arms and the sleeping lions in Trafalgar Square. With 1992 on the near horizon (on the far side of the 300th anniversary of the Battle of the Boyne in 1990 with all that entails for relations between Britain and Ireland and between Britain and the Papacy) we have to face not only a new commercial and political relationship with western Europe, but implications for the Church and the Monarchy as well as Parliament. What is to be the future role of the British Lion, the Monarchy and Parliament with its control of the armed forces and the police and the judiciary and our relationship with the Commonwealth as well as Europe? It is time for us to consider such questions now before all our institutions are shaken to their roots.

As conflicts between principalities and powers rise to a crescendo, leading to a possible financial crash and civil unrest, even world conflict, which more and more people see as a dark cloud much bigger than a man's hand no longer on the far distant horizon, we need to consider what makes for unity, peace and renewal rather than chaos. This means coming to know not just of the unity between

Financial crash, civil unrest, even world conflict ... we need to value silence and the indwelling Spirit of God. The times demand an end to all forms of fundamentalism

cherubim and seraphim which we sing about in the *Te Deum* but to know to love and worship and adore the Trinity. The love relationship between the Father-Mother, Son and Holy Spirit goes beyond arguments about a male-only priesthood but gives hope of a Church in which Catholic and Evangelical elements can combine with others who value silence and the indwelling Spirit of God, without which we cannot know the One God who is over and beyond all, through all, and in all. The times we live in demand an end to all forms of fundamentalism, whether Catholic or Protestant, and a combination between the prophetic insights of Fr Gilbert Shaw and Fr Jim Wilson with Evangelical spirituality. From the ruins of Glastonbury Abbey comes a prophetic message not of ruin and destruction but of hope for those prepared to follow the way of the Cross into the Kingdom of God.

> From the ruins of Glastonbury Abbey comes a prophetic message not of destruction but of hope for those prepared to follow the way of the Cross

During 1988 contact with the Acorn Christian Healing Trust and the Divine Healing Mission had to be somewhat curtailed but opportunities continued to relate to Benedictines at Buckfast Abbey and Downside and there was time for initiatives connected with the Guild of Health in the southwest and nationally. As 1989 opens, God seems to be drawing a number of people to Glastonbury where the way ahead is becoming clearer. At the right time his purposes will unfold.

January 1990

Sixth Glastonbury Newsletter

Glimpses of the world — 1989

A powerful spontaneous upsurge of dissent and nationalism in eastern Europe led to the overthrow, at least for the time being, of Leninist Stalinist oppressors. A measure of co-operation between the Soviet Union, the United States, Britain and western Europe has made for reduced tension in many parts of the world. There has been a major move towards German and European reunification which included the breaching of the Berlin Wall. Economic barriers have been partly dismantled as unarmed multitudes defied tyrannies and gained a measure of freedom (except in China). Attempts have been made to suppress the drug trade but little attention has yet been given to correcting the economic factors, including exploitation by rich nations, which give rise to production of drugs by impoverished farmers in the Third World.

In Britain the government has sought to correct the balance between the southeast and other parts of the country by developing industry in the north of England, Scotland, Wales and Northern Ireland, but defeat of the Provisional IRA remains a distant dream. Arguments about education, the health service, nuclear power, green issues, unemployment and training people for jobs, as well as homelessness, continue; some concessions have been made, but the gulf between rich and poor remains deep and wide.

Glastonbury

The churches remain on the fringe of community life, though the time for involvement is perhaps becoming nearer; only when the somewhat complacent and comfortable lifestyle of those reasonably well off is threatened do people stir in any numbers. A minority look for spiritual renewal during the Decade of Evangelism in the 1990s and see the need for the churches to come alive. The gulf between the world consciousness of the Alternatives, who see a new world and a new age coming, and the dormant nationalism and group loyalty of the churches continues; there is deep-seated resistance to change. Thus the main difference is less between the churches and the remainder of the community than between the majority in the community and the Alternatives.

Attempts to bridge the gulf are being made. On the one hand, there are those in the churches who are becoming aware of the healing power of Christ and, on the other, those outside the churches involved with drugs and black magic are becoming more open as evil and good grow towards the harvest. If there is a growing sense in the churches of belonging to a body of people with a still largely undefined purpose, younger people find vitality in the fundamentalist community church or the Alternatives, both of which think they have found something spiritually the churches do not have. The former believe in sin and forgiveness; the latter in "the cosmic Christ" in creation together with karma, reincarnation, respect for mother earth, earth energies, elemental spirits, astrology, contact with spirits and the sacredness and equality of life — issues which most churchpeople with our hierarchical church structure have never considered. The Decade of Evangelism will expose the weakness of a faith which does not take other religions

Cosmic Christ, creation, karma, reincarnation, mother earth, elemental spirits, sacredness of life, astrology — issues most churchpeople never consider seriously, though a faithful remnant will emerge in the churches and outside, including bishops, priests and ministers, to face the spiritual challenge which is coming.

The Abbey, Anglicanism and local churches

If the Abbey is still more of a museum than a dynamic spiritual centre, regular weekly services of Holy Communion continue, either in St Patrick's chapel (one of two medieval hospice chapels) or, in summer, in the crypt chapel dedicated to St Joseph of Arimathea under the floorless and roofless Lady chapel. The Abbey bookshop, now under the control of the Abbey trustees, has become more of a Christian centre to be incorporated into the first stage of the new entrance complex shortly to be opened. During 1989 the "Abbey Chapter" — consisting of Anglican clergy and lay readers — came into being; currently activities are confined to daily evensong in St John's Church but it is hoped that eventually volunteer clergy will meet visitors to the Abbey. Sadly there is as yet no shared control with and little participation by the Roman or Free Churches; the time is perhaps not yet ripe. Growth in the number of prayer and study groups in the churches, some ecumenical, is encouraging, links with Anglican Franciscans have become stronger.

> The Abbey is still more of a museum than a dynamic spiritual centre. But growth in prayer and study groups in the churches is encouraging

Assembly Rooms

During 1989 attempts have been made to place the administration of the Assembly Rooms on a sounder foundation to support a programme which includes many events such as the dance festival, plays — many about social, moral, psychical and spiritual truth, workshops, discos, and a variety of social events. These in the main attract mostly Alternatives, who value anything which transcends national, social, class and cultural divisions and contains an element of dissent. In such areas the Assembly Rooms, for all its faults, is way ahead of the churches. The "coordinator" appointed for one year from November

1988 with the help of grants from Community Education and the Grail Trust has been replaced by an administrator, paid by being responsible for a youth training scheme centred on the Assembly Rooms. This strengthens contacts with Workface [a local training agency] and the Glastonbury Dance Festival.

Interest charges on the £40,000 bank loan required to purchase the premises from Somerset county council escalated during the year by some 40 percent. Attempts are being made to find ways and means of lowering the cost, which depends on ensuring a better decision-making process and getting the right balance between paid staff, for whom funds are required, and volunteers, who have played a vital role in getting the venture started. The struggle for survival continues and, although as yet there is little real support from the churches, there is a dawning recognition that something important for Glastonbury as a world spiritual centre is happening at the Assembly Rooms.

In January 1989 an opportunity came to introduce a gospel singer (of negro and other spirituals) of international repute, based at Assisi, Italy. In July the Revd Donald Reeves of St James's Piccadilly came to speak about developments there, prior to speaking the following day at the Chalice Well; both meetings were well attended by both Alternatives and church people. At the July meeting there was a confrontation with a posse from the Mid-Somerset Community Church who pray against the Assembly Rooms and regard it as satanic. This brought into the open a firmly Christian element among the Alternatives and led to a gentle stand by some churchpeople willing to stand up and be counted, who hold a very different version of the Christian faith from hardline fundamentalism.

A posse who pray against what they regard as satanic led to a gentle stand by some churchpeople willing to stand up and be counted

Homelessness

Memories of the Greenlands situation and a small minority of socially disruptive travellers and local troublemakers have made provision of facilities for homeless and travelling young people difficult. It does not even make it any easier to meet the needs of local residents for housing which, partly due to government policy, is growing; more and more families are having to go into temporary accommodation or into "bread and breakfast" for as much as six months.

Vociferous local people who feel threatened whip up opposition and a few descend to violence against isolated individuals; little or nothing is done to relieve social problems which get Glastonbury a bad name. Nevertheless an Action for Homes group for Street and Glastonbury with strong Quaker backing was founded during 1989. County and district councillors and employees see the need for more to be done in and around Glastonbury, but it seems that a growing price must be paid for the failure of the Abbey to fulfil its medieval role and for the weakness of the churches, which inevitably find it difficult to face a challenge which many prefer to ignore.

The Alternatives

During the year the Glastonbury Experience, which has had financial and other problems but has sought to make more room for the Christian dimension, has become more stabilized. Interest in natural and psychic healing and "rebirthing" go hand in hand with commercial interests; bodies like the Wrekin Trust and people like Sir George Trevelyan are never far away as the search for peace apart from Christian dogmatism continues. The Avalon Library, founded in 1988, launched a major and ambitious appeal for funds during the year with Professor James Carley, author of a new authoritative book on Glastonbury Abbey, as president, and the Bishop of Bath and Wells as vice-president. This makes for a link between the Church and the Alternatives, but the question remains how much support will be forthcoming. Renting premises from Glastonbury Experience is the Shambala bookshop, which is a cover for a "maitreya" or, in Alternative terms, a false Christ.

Many false Christs of various kinds are attracted to Glastonbury

Many false Christs of various kinds are attracted to Glastonbury and during the year there has been growth in the number of people practising black magic and Satanism with full rituals. A wider-than-Glastonbury conference was held at the

Abbey House during the year on the subject of deliverance ministry, which was ecumenical and much appreciated by Anglicans and members of other denominations. Several premises sited in the area of Glastonbury below St John's Church are infested and steps need to be taken to make a well informed stand, remembering that Christian fundamentalism may aggravate rather than help. A few individual church members, some who have come from the Alternative background, are involved in this area.

Wider links

A visit to Wales enabled renewed contact with Canon Norman Autton of Cardiff, who is well aware of the importance of Celtic creation and Trinitarian spirituality; he will shortly be retiring and has much to contribute. This was followed by a stay in Scotland with the Revd Martin Reith, a priest in the Scottish Episcopal Church in the hermitic tradition, and several days at Bishop's House, Iona, which included contact with Iona Abbey. A conference in 1991 is being planned to develop links between Glastonbury and Iona, drawing on deep Catholic and Christian roots. It will probably take place June 1–8 at Bishop's House. Perhaps this can help in bridging the gulf between science and religion, psychical and spiritual truth, town and country, and between the classes — so necessary for a middle-class Church like the Church in England.

Bridging the gulf between science and religion, psychic and spiritual, town and country and between the classes

Following the arrival of Canon Charles Shells in Glastonbury — he was for many years at Bristol Cathedral — a link-up has been made with the Revd Tom Curtis Hayward, a Roman Catholic priest from Stroud, who has friends amongst the Druids likely to be attracted to Glastonbury. There followed a conference at Prinknash Abbey in August involving Druids, Freemasons and British Israelites. Whilst a common base emerged in Celtic spirituality it became clear how little many of the participants knew of the spiritual tradition to which they claimed to belong; a group is now meeting in Glastonbury and a follow-up conference is planned for July 1990. Hopefully this will help us communicate with those outside the churches involved with creation theology and with natural powers including magic, and to improve the quality and effectiveness of the churches' ministry of deliverance so much needed in Glastonbury, at Stonehenge, and at events like the Pilton pop festival.

During the year a visit was paid to the Pilsdon Community in Dorset with a group of praying people, mostly related to the Guild of Health; this renewed contact with the Revd Stuart Affleck, the warden, who has much to contribute to the Glastonbury scene, and is into Celtic insights, and is aware of the need for the churches to transcend class barriers.

Membership of a small ARCIC [Anglican–Roman Catholic International Commission] group which includes several monks from Downside Abbey proved that openness to the Celtic dimension with its rejection of authoritarianism is to be found within the Roman Catholic Church on a wider basis than many might expect.

Openness to the Celtic, with its rejection of authoritarianism, is more widely found within the Catholic Church than many expect

Due to the initiative of the Revd Jonathan Robinson, founder of the Grail Trust, becoming known as a retreat conductor, it proved possible to meet Canon Peter Spink, prior of the Omega Community at Winford Manor and a notable exponent of New Age spirituality. He knew Marjorie Milne and is interested in Glastonbury. Jonathan Robinson is shortly to leave Stoke St Gregory, where he has been vicar for some years, and plans to move to the Monmouth area. He has already made a link with the Welsh Church and opened a centre in Abergenolwyn, near Tywyn, for communicating creation spirituality and the Christian faith to the younger generation, who find existing church structures and worship difficult. Hopefully this will bring renewed links with Bishop Stephen Verney and others in the Oxford area as part of something wider happening in the life of the British Church.

Following the move of the Anglican Benedictine community from Nashdom to Elmore Abbey and renewed contact with the Mirfield Community through Fr Luke CR, the time may be coming ripe to follow up some of the contacts which stem from the Greenbus project of the late 1960s, with its roots in the desire of young people for renewed spiritual vigour, which led to community involvement in Glastonbury during the early 1970s until [the unpleasant end of] Greenlands brought such cooperation to a stop. Brother (not Father) Jeremy CR paid a welcome return visit to Glastonbury during the year from South Africa.

Thus the commencement of a new decade will see the way clearer for the emerging of an ecumenical Christian community in Glastonbury which will tackle the extraordinary range of spiritual and natural forces which home in here and make it a place of conflict at a time when Glastonbury, Britain, Europe and the whole world are in a state of flux. Perhaps we in the churches are slowly becoming more like pilgrims on the move even if, like Abraham, we do not know where we are going. The 1990s will be a time of challenge and opportunity. Glimpses of the world at the beginning of this newsletter reveal that the world needs the Christian Church even if in Britain it is still largely middle-class, patronizing to those outside and to other denominations and therefore unable to reach out to others and bridge the gulfs which exist in contemporary society, so suspicious of much of the Christian Church. It seems that no major move forward will come until the churches in Glastonbury are ready to start caring for those outside and have an impact on the life of the community.

January 1991

Seventh Glastonbury Newsletter

As the world changes ever more rapidly, sadly the Christian Church has communicated the faith once delivered to the Saints in a form irrelevant to the majority of the people of Britain. At the end of 1990 we face the prospect of major armed conflict in the Middle East, the Soviet Union appears to be drifting towards breakup, and Germany is emerging as the major power in western Europe. More than three hundred years after Boers landed in Cape Town and King William III crossed the Boyne, South Africa and Northern Ireland are in a state of conflict, and the Church is having to come to grips with the ancient religions of Egypt, India and China (as well as Hebrew, Latin and Greek), which enshrine truths lost or submerged for centuries, at a time when our nation is in danger of losing freedom under Common Law and the Magna Carta to a remote European bureaucracy.

No wonder there is a crisis of authority not only in a middle-class Church torn with male–female arguments but in a nation in which the 17th-century settlement between Monarchy and Parliament is increasingly called into question. How much we need the Christian hope that light shines in darkness and the darkness cannot overcome it.

In Glastonbury, the finger of the ruined tower of St

75

Much of the Church seems concerned only with personal morality and not with the corporate sin of groups and society

Michael's chapel on top of the Tor stands as a promise that St Michael, or Christ himself, will return and the psychic morass of confusion and destruction associated with earth energies — with air, fire and water out of control — will, with the principalities and powers of the universe, be brought to praise and magnify God so that harmony can be restored. At a time when much of the Church seems concerned only with personal morality and not with the corporate sin of groups and society, Christianity seems clapped out — not God's answer for a world and universe groaning in pain which needs turning upside-down, as happened in the days of the early Church. It can happen — it will happen, but through all the argument, when the Son of Man comes, will he find faith on earth?

Rosemary and James have now been more than ten years in Glastonbury, years during which the spiritual battle has intensified. New life has begun to come to the churches even if there are setbacks and there is still preference for party or denominational spirituality which seeks to limit the Holy Spirit to church structures and church buildings and to limited areas of life. We forget that wind or water contained in a vessel go stale, whilst fire, deprived of air, smoulders and goes out. Charismatic renewal, creation, new-age theology make for movement and change but uncorrected can become demonic — there can be growth but it may be cancerous, and power struggles may intensify. In 1990 Glastonbury churches began to consider covenanting for unity unattainable through the cheap grace which people desire without holiness. Maybe 1991 will see the emergence of deeper Christian hope, and denominations will give up power games. As yet there is little sign that this will happen.

The Abbey and the Tor

The first stage of the new entrance complex to the Abbey was completed during the year; it may do much to attract middle-class tourist business but does little to enhance the prestige of the Abbey amongst Alternatives, who see in it one more sign of a decadent middle-class church unable to communicate the Gospel to the poor. Alternatives look to earth energies and were encouraged by John Michell's book *New light on the Ancient Mysteries of Glastonbury*, launched in the Gothic Image bookshop. This book links Glastonbury with pagan and druidic mystery religions, with power associated with the moon, the sun, earth energies and the zodiac, with dragon or serpent lines, with male and female fertility cults, with massive earthworks and stone-age relics of megalithic society antedating Abraham. At key sites these "ley lines" of natural power meet or cross each other, the point of intersection sometimes being the high altar of important ancient churches, cathedrals and abbeys, including Glastonbury Abbey. On the Tor two such lines connected with "gods" merge or combine, as they do at Avebury or possibly Stonehenge, probably to increase fertility.

> The medieval Church 'baptized' natural energies to ensure they were rightly used and to prevent abuse of power

The medieval Church "baptized" these energies, linking them with St Michael or the Blessed Virgin Mary, to ensure they were rightly used so that abuse of power was prevented. At present there is abuse of power in and around Glastonbury, which needs attention by the Church.

A Church which neglects these energies or natural powers, ignores them or condemns them as evil, has much to learn from Alternatives. Many Christians will find this view unpalatable; nevertheless these powers are being released, and Christians need to be on guard so they may be brought under God, Jesus Christ and the Holy Spirit. To condemn, as fundamentalists do, is not the way of Christ and leads to tensions and divisions within the Church. Any covenant for unity by local churches should take such factors into account, and so should the Abbey Trustees and the Abbey Development Trust, if Glastonbury Abbey is to be resurrected in a form compatible with the 21st century. Spiritual warfare is hotting up and the Church needs to prepare for it.

Benedictines and Franciscans

A place as unstable as Glastonbury needs the soundly based open spirituality found in well established religious communities as support for local churches and congregations less spiritually aware. Benedictines and Franciscans, whether Anglicans or Roman Catholic, have a special role. A visit to Elmore Abbey, the new home of Anglican monks from Nashdom, proved of value; at present they are consolidating their home base and attracting new members, but involvement in the affairs of Glastonbury is not for them as it was some years ago; contact to exchange information will continue.

A place as unstable as Glastonbury needs the soundly based open spirituality of established religious communities

Contact is also maintained with monks from Downside through involvement with an ARCIC group [Anglican–Roman Catholic International Commission]. Some of them are aware of the Celtic dimension and of creation theology, which means they have much to offer the sections of the Christian Church seeking to relate to Alternatives.

Liaison continues between churchpeople in Glastonbury and the Franciscan sisters at Compton Durville, which assists those seeking a soundly based prayer life, and also with Hilfield Friary. Brother Bernard (now sadly experiencing ill health) moved to London; his successor Brother Victor suggested a link between Glastonbury and Warminster, which is being followed up in 1991, to help ensure that action related to Alternatives is rightly based.

The "new age"

The main intellectual centres for the New Age in Glastonbury continue to be at the Chalice Well, Gothic Image and the Glastonbury Experience, with the addition of Isis, started by Baroness Isi van Coels from Germany. Gradually there is coming into this area of spirituality an increasing awareness of the importance of Christ and also of the man Jesus, which can make for conflict. It is perhaps wiser not to say much about this, as the issues it raises are far from restricted to Glastonbury. The year 1991 should see further developments here, which has implications for both houses of Parliament and the Royal Family, as the foundations of our national life are increasingly shaken, until only that which is of God survives.

Assembly Rooms

During the year the crisis facing the Assembly Rooms intensified, partly due to government cutbacks involving community education, partly due to high bank interest on a loan for £40,000, partly due to inefficient administration and to personality clashes, which make the task of any administrator seeking to combine community arts and other activities with care for unemployed people and travellers difficult if not impossible. The trustees of the Rooms found it essential to expose the true situation of the "Friends", many of whom had lost interest.

Whilst thanks to a most generous donation the café was reconstructed and opened under new management, income from rents and hirings proved inadequate to balance the books; the former was partly corrected by the Trust, the latter — for which the Friends were responsible — were not. To avert substantial personal loss for guarantors of the bank loan, the Trustees gave notice to terminate the agency agreement with the Friends and set up an interim management committee pending the sale of the building or its transfer to a body of people who would run it as a community centre.

An attempt to form a committee to tackle homelessness failed for lack of community support

Various other steps, including the setting up of a drop-in centre with wider backing, is being considered. An attempt to form a committee of people, which had some church support, to tackle homelessness amongst young people failed for lack of adequate community support. The whole local community — including the churches, the Abbey, the town council, the Chamber of Commerce and the district council with special responsibility for homelessness — need to take note of the need for strengthening the body of people involved with the Assembly Rooms, instead of falling for the propaganda of those who blame the Assembly Rooms for all Glastonbury's ills. On the right basis the Assembly Rooms, provided some of the pressures are removed, could be in a unique position to reconcile conflicting elements in Glastonbury's society, as well as being a base for community arts. The primary victory has already been won on the Cross.

King Arthur and Celtic spirituality

One of the encouraging developments during the year stemmed from contact with Mrs Elizabeth Leader, of the Research into Lost Knowledge Organization. Books she introduced included *The High History of the Holy Grail* and *The Temple of the Stars*. Read at the right stage, these books help us understand how part of the medieval Church, in particular Celtic monks and writers, coped with tyranny and helped preserve a spirituality less corrupted by power games than that associated with St Augustine of Hippo and his namesake of Canterbury, and St Wilfrid.

At first sight this may seem unimportant now, but when such insights are linked with Welsh and Scottish spirituality it becomes evident that the Arthurian legends keep alive a tradition in which the king shares in the suffering and hardships of his people, evil is fought, life is lived in harmony with God and with natural creation in a way which makes for fertility of the soil and right use of powers connected with earth, air, fire and water and with the spirit world (which we seek to express in the Communion of Saints), all related to the One God revealed through the Christ of creation. As with Matthew Fox, creation is seen as in origin good and not evil and yet redeemed through grace. As those of other faiths and the Alternatives point out, Western Christians have gone seriously wrong in these areas. We need to be more honest about the evil in our past, more humble, more open to truth in Christ, willing to learn from people on whose cherished beliefs and holy ground we have often trodden with contempt.

At the 1989 conference of Christians, Pagans and Druids held at Prinknash Grange, Fr Tom Curtis Hayward (a Roman Catholic priest for years in the Avebury–Stonehenge area) told of the Iona legend about St Oran. This legend preserves in another form the Welsh belief that King Arthur will return. Both these legends are ways of keeping alive scientific and political truth which for Celts were part of their religious belief. The time has now come ripe for understanding such truths submerged for centuries, now surfacing outside of the Church amongst those who reject the materialist way of life which has enslaved much of the Church. This led to progress in mutual understanding which will present a growing challenge to fundamentalists in the Church, whether "Catholic" or "Protestant", help us link up with our Celtic spiritual inheritance, and enable the Church to give spiritual counsel to the "New Age".

> Such truths are surfacing amongst those who reject the materialist way of life which has enslaved so much of the Church

The deeper we go the more we find in the Celtic dimension Indo-European roots, not only in the fertile crescent of the Nile, the Tigris and the Euphrates, but in the ancient megalithic civilization of the Indus valley with its Aryan associations of the master race, amongst whom the "King" was seen as God incarnate. Modern archaeology aided by people like Thor Heyerdahl open the way for us to link this knowledge up with heraldry, with the lion, the bull, the eagle and the man, and with the Biblical cherubim. This area becomes demonic especially when the feminine is repressed and coercion becomes the norm in a male-dominated society.

The Grail Trust

1990 saw the Revd Jonathan Robinson, who has spent some years as Anglican incumbent at Stoke St Gregory (where King Alfred lived for a time before emerging to conquer the Danes and converting them to Christ), resign and move with his family to Monmouth. Helped by local contacts he has opened a centre for retreats at Abergenolwyn, near Tywyn, central Wales. Jonathan Robinson has links with India and has had contact with Fr Bede Griffiths and is aware of the relevance of Celtic spirituality for today. This move led to a meeting between the Trustees of the Grail Trust and members of various Welsh churches in the area at which all found a meeting point in Celtic spirituality — Christ-centred and fully Trinitarian — related to the life and work of ordinary people, not just for popes, Church potentates or hierarchical kings, not just for the middle classes or for those who insist that they alone have the right to tell others how to behave or what to believe.

Linked with deep undercurrents in Welsh spirituality and with legend, as well as Scottish and Irish Celtic insights, poetic prophetic truth and myth are not understood by many English scholars, who are blinded by their tradition. Fundamentalists see the Celtic approach as betraying "Christian values"; others can perhaps learn to draw on such insights and help prepare the way for renewal and outreach of far greater significance than what has happened in the last thirty years towards the healing, not just of individuals, but of families, the Church, the nation and the land, including departed spirits. This gives point to the direction in which the Grail Trust is going.

... to heal not just individuals, but families, the Church, the nation and the land, including departed spirits

Christian healing, renewal and reconciliation

During 1990 renewed contact came with Brian Frost, author of *Glastonbury Journey* and *An Unknown Glastonbury Mystic*, happily recovering from a serious illness. Brian is concerned with the social dimension of healing, the politics of forgiveness, the Green movement, and the peace and justice movement, which stands firm where there is abuse of power by those in positions of authority in Church or state.

Also during 1990, James gave up the chair of Guild of Health committees meeting in Devon and Dorset but has continued to seek to draw together various agencies of Christian healing, including the Acorn Christian Healing Trust, the Guild of Health, the Churches' Fellowship for Psychical and Spiritual Studies, and the Divine Healing Mission — sometimes locally, sometimes nationally. Interest in developing the Christian healing ministry at Buckfast Abbey continued but sadly, on the last day of the year, a telephone call was received from Mrs Christine Jones from Buckfastleigh reporting the sudden death of her husband Eric, who played the major role developing this ministry in conjunction with the Abbot of Buckfast.

Awareness of the Celtic contribution towards Christian healing and wholeness was strengthened by the 1989 visit of Rosemary and James to the Revd Martin Reith, the Episcopal Church of Scotland priest-hermit who has been given profound Celtic poetic and prophetic insights into natural creation and the historical dimension of Scottish spirituality — which has given more to England than is acknowledged and has more to give *now*.

Plans have been made for a conference or pilgrimage to Iona in June 1991, which should bring together people from Glastonbury with the Guild of Health council and with Episcopal and Presbyterian priests and ministers from Scotland, from whom we in England have much to learn. In this, which is to be based on Bishop's House, the Iona Community has a part to play to help us in England draw on spiritual riches of which too little is known, so we may approach closer to the fullness of Christ.

We will be able to face the psychic and spirit dimensions without fear, as all is brought under the sovereignty of Christ

Thus in 1990 there is emerging hope that the Church in England will eventually meet the challenge of class, race, sex and religious conflict, natural science, the Green movement, and truths in other faiths which give rise to New Age spirituality. Perhaps we will be able to face the psychic and spirit dimensions without fear as all is brought under the sovereignty of Christ — science, mathematics and numbers, politics, philosophy, music, creation and redemption, all peoples and all nations again under the One God, as before the fall. In 1990 people all over the world have been moving in that direction; Jesus the Christ can return to save the world and not to condemn it.

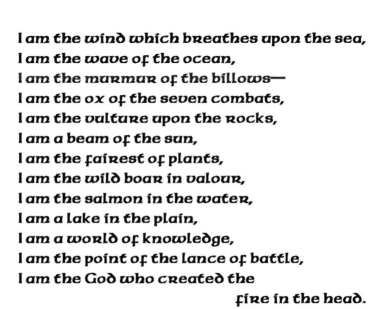

I am the wind which breathes upon the sea,
I am the wave of the ocean,
I am the murmur of the billows—
I am the ox of the seven combats,
I am the vulture upon the rocks,
I am a beam of the sun,
I am the fairest of plants,
I am the wild boar in valour,
I am the salmon in the water,
I am a lake in the plain,
I am a world of knowledge,
I am the point of the lance of battle,
I am the God who created the
                                fire in the head.

This is traditionally believed to be the first poem ever composed in Ireland. There is no dualism here. All is one. This ancient poem pre-empts and reverses the lonely helplessness of Descartes' "*Cogito ergo sum* — I think, therefore I am." To the Celtic poet, I am because everything else is. I am in everything and everything is in me.

From *Anam Cara: spiritual wisdom from the Celtic World*
by John O'Donohue

84

12 September 1919 – 5 September 1998

James Turnbull:
a brief biography

by Rosemary Turnbull

Born near Chelmsford in Essex, James grew up first at Hildersham near Cambridge, later moved to Maidstone and then Tunbridge Wells in Kent, where he was at Tonbridge School until 17 years old. He then went to work with Plant Protection, a subsidiary of ICI. Having been in the Officer

Training Corps at school (the cadet at far right in this photo), he was called up in August 1939, shortly before war broke out, to serve in the

Royal Artillery. He began army life as a Second Lieutenant and became a Captain at the age of just 21.

In 1941 he was posted abroad and served under General Montgomery in the Middle East and Africa. He took part in the Italian landing at Anzio, and was mentioned in despatches and later awarded the Distinguished Service Medal in 1945. At the end of the war, he was in Germany responsible for 12,000 prisoners of war, with only a thin band of barbed wire and fifty soldiers to contain them.

Returning to Tunbridge Wells, he went back to work for ICI in London. We met in 1948 — I was Rosemary Robertson then — and married on 23 October. We honeymooned at Lake Como in Italy, and on our return James was sent to America for four months' research. In 1951 we were moved to York and then to Bramhall, Manchester, where James was in charge of the agricultural side of ICI for the north. During this period two of our children were born: Christopher James in 1950 and Catherine in 1953.

At the age of 36, James experienced a "calling" to the priesthood and decided to leave ICI. In April 1956 he went to see Bishop George Bell of Chichester

about the possibility of ordination in the Church of England. Bishop Bell confirmed that James had a vocation as a priest and volunteered to arrange his training without any necessity to go through the usual selection conference. ICI insisted on a year's notice, as someone would have to be trained to take over James's very senior job.

James went to St Augustine's College, Canterbury, to prepare for the ministry and was ordained on 1 June 1958, Trinity Sunday. He served his title at St Peter's Brighton, where Canon Peter Booth was the vicar. In 1960 while in Brighton our third child was born, Martin.

On 27 February 1961 James was instituted and inducted to be Vicar of Sayers Common and Rector of Twineham, two country parishes ten miles north of Brighton, where we spent the next 14½ years. He was also chaplain of an approved school and of an isolation hospital.

Then on 15 July 1975 James was licensed to the living of St Julian's, Kingston Buci (part of Shoreham-by-Sea), just west of Brighton. There he was required to bring understanding between a charismatic group and traditional church worshippers. This was achieved — thanks be to God!

But we were both exhausted and needed a rest, so in 1980 we moved to Glastonbury. By then the two older children were both married — Christopher living in the Wirral and Catherine near Glastonbury — and Martin married in 1982. When James died in 1998 he had eight grandchildren.

He spent his eighteen years in Glastonbury helping out in local churches and relating to those outside the church structures and living an alternative lifestyle. He became a trusted spiritual guide to seekers and leaders in varied walks of life. James was, as is written on a plaque under a holly tree dedicated to him in the grounds of Glastonbury Abbey:

A prophetic and deeply caring man who brought reconciliation and was much loved.

January 1992

Eighth Glastonbury Newsletter

Cry for the Church in England

For forty years since 1951 Britain has been taking the wrong road. The result is corruption in high places, massive unemployment, increased crime against property, homelessness, lying, cheating, poll tax evasion, affecting millions of people. Abuse of power by the state — fearing appeasement of dissidents as at Stonehenge and in our inner cities — has increased latent hostility to the police. As in South Africa when Alan Paton wrote *Cry the Beloved Country*, politicians of all parties seek materialist solutions to a deep spiritual disease, reminding us of the decline and fall of ancient Egypt or the Roman Empire. The world, the flesh and the devil rampage, and if we are not vigilant the way will open up for dictatorship. Even if there is a measure of renewal in the churches they are still like salt which has lost its savour — fit only to be spat out and trodden under foot.

We have not been without modern equivalents of Elijah or John the Baptist with their call to repentance and a moral lead with its roots in Jewish, Christian and Islamic law, but the time for that is now past — aggressive fundamentalism is not truly spiritual. In 1991 many who seek a spiritual answer look for

Jesus in the churches, but they see him only in people like Mother Teresa or Terry Waite; in the Church of England they see concern for finance, clergy stipends, repair of ancient buildings and revival meetings, which condemn New Agers and many others as evil.

Glastonbury and the Church of the future

In this situation Glastonbury is a potential focal point for reconciliation, but only when a Christian form emerges which is beyond English or Roman Catholic power games associated with empire or world dominance by the Papacy and the Vatican. A vital truth learnt from 22 years of parochial ministry and 11 years in Glastonbury is that a historical point of conflict not only between Christian denominations (and C of E parties) but, as C. S. Lewis has shown, between Christians and those of other faiths including honest pagans and even "atheists" can become a focal point for reconciliation.

A historical point of conflict can become a focal point for reconciliation

On our arrival in 1980 the Anglican Church was divided against itself as was the Methodist Church. The struggle between the Roman Catholic and the Anglican Church, between the Crown and the Papacy, was reflected in the Abbey and in the RC shrine as recently as the early 1960s, the time of the Second Vatican Council. In part this is a hangover from the judicial murder of Abbot Richard Whiting and two of his monks on the Tor. As yet forgiveness is only skin-deep and people say "peace, peace" where there is no peace. Brian Frost, who wrote the biography of Marjorie Milne, seeks to remedy this in his book *The Politics of Peace*, mainly for situations outside of Britain as a pointer to the way forward. True peace cannot come so long as Anglican clergy are dependent on handouts from the Church Commissioners in a country ruled by Mammon, where the RC and Evangelical Protestant churches seek to impose doctrines (even heretical doctrines) on all Christians as the price of a bogus unity which can never be.

No wonder that James who, over a period of eleven years has endeavoured to ensure that such issues are faced, has met opposition and faced blocks to action even if, with the help of sympathetic and understanding clergy, he has played a minor role in the Anglican Church and in the local Council of Churches whilst relating, as requested by Bishop John Bickersteth before the Turnbulls moved to Glastonbury, to what proved to be an explosive situation at Greenlands Farm. Add to this the controversial Pilton pop festival and the Alternatives — rent asunder like the churches with conflicts personal, cultural and theological — James faced inevitable opposition from people, including clergy, who felt threatened. One result was that he was barred from clergy and doctor–clergy fraternals. He has never been invited to report on his work to the Anglican Ruri-Decanal Synod, of which Rosemary is an ex-officio member.

This is being written now in the hope that when the Revd John Sumner and his wife Alice move to Glastonbury to found a community, hopefully of the kind foreseen by Marjorie Milne, they do not have to face similar opposition but cooperation and support from churches which recognize that they are unable to meet the spiritual needs of many people. This does not mean that individual clergy and laypeople have been unsupportive — and to them warm and grateful thanks is extended. Perhaps the heart of the difficulty which the churches in England have in meeting contemporary needs is that they have not yet learnt to draw on spiritual riches of early Christian Celtic insights, which have been suppressed in England both by those in power here and in Rome, as part of an attempt during the last two thousand years to destroy Celtic culture, languages and religious faith and impose a hierarchical system alien to Celts, and also by taking over myths never properly understood.

The heart of the difficulty which Churches in England have in meeting today's needs is that they do not draw on spiritual riches of early Celtic Christians

Hope for the Church

Celtic culture and spirituality is now re-emerging in Britain and Ireland and on the continents of Europe and America. In June 1991 twenty-four of us, including twelve priests or ministers of various denominations, explored this dimension on the island of Iona. The conference was seen to provide the key to help us break free of religious and political fundamentalism with its potential for tyranny as expressed in the Spanish and Tudor inquisitions. It must be centred on the uniqueness of Christ, for when it goes wrong it re-emerges with IRA, UVF and Basque violence. There are dark forces around and woe betide us if we forget it. Hope for the future would seem to lie in an understanding between the [Celtic and the] Latin–Greek tradition as introduced by St Augustine of Canterbury, St Wilfrid and others in which each respects the other and neither seeks to dominate.

There is no space here to share the insights of a whole week's conference reported in the October issue of the Churches' Council for Health and Healing magazine *Health and Healing* [see Appendix, page 161] and to the whole of the January–March issue of the Guild of Health magazine *Way of Life*, which contains a summary of most of the main talks. Suffice to say that Celts see the whole creation — natural, spiritual and celestial worlds — as parts of one order and see second sight into the spiritual world as acceptable. For Benedictine insistence on poverty, chastity and obedience, the Celtic monastic tradition values humility, patience and love. Insight into truth is poetic, prophetic and mystical, as expressed in an oral tradition which relies on visual images rather than abstract truth, and appeals to people who work with their hands and to scientists, not just to people who value natural justice, moral law and Greek philosophy. Different national expressions tend to hold part of the truth which is so much bigger than any of us.

Assembly Rooms

Fear of massive traveller invasions still grips much of Glastonbury [where locals still use the word "hippies" to refer to them]. The cliff-hanging situation caused by stress felt by those who work in the Assembly Rooms, coupled with financial stress, came to an end when some 80 or more people each subscribed £500 in cash or by means of a loan from Mercury Provident — a less Mammon-oriented body than banks or building societies. The great strength of the Assembly Rooms has been as an international centre where people meet regardless of class, colour, race or creed, where men and women are equals. Unemployed people, homeless people, people with mental breakdowns and socially deprived people, some very difficult, have been made welcome by people who worked for a pittance or for nothing. The strain has been enormous and the new venture can no longer act as a drop-in centre; all the churches and the wider community have a responsibility which is not being met. Having had the main financial responsibility for four and a half years, James is now free of that anxiety and is more able to give time to Christian pastoral care and guidance for people who rarely, if ever, darken the doors of the churches.

Alternatives

If the Alternatives have a major say in the Assembly Rooms and draw much inspiration from centres like the Glastonbury Experience and the Gothic Image, they help to provide a necessary balance in Glastonbury. They help the churches to avoid an unhealthy attachment to Christian fundamentalism and unhealthy fear of magic and the psychic dimension, which makes a healthy respect for natural science difficult if not impossible; they can also help us break free of our slavery to Mammon.

One of the Alternatives is Serena Roney-Dougal, who has both second sight and a PhD in parapsychology; she is widely used as an exorcist and has written a number of books. Early in life she fell foul of RC priests and rejected the false view of Christ with which she was presented. Many men and women have become feminists like her, having had similar conflicts with Anglican priests or Free Church ministers, especially if they have suffered male child abuse. For some, discovery of the white

> Alternatives help the churches avoid unhealthy fundamentalism and can also help us break free of our slavery to Mammon

goddess has been a liberation: they have seen the light which to those who believe in a male-only God is of darkness and of Satan.

Children's World, the registered charity started by Arabella Churchill, celebrated its tenth anniversary with an outdoor party in the Abbey Park for up to 1500 children; many came with parents. That event gave James, who is a trustee, an opportunity to use a version of the Lord's Prayer beginning Father-Mother God without causing the conflict such use would cause in a Glastonbury church, even if both St Francis and Mother Julian of Norwich used that term.

Both St Francis and Mother Julian of Norwich used the term "Father-Mother God"

During 1991 both John Michell and Hamish Miller have had books published after investigation into natural powers connected with churches named after St Michael and the Blessed Virgin Mary, with Glastonbury churches, the Abbey, the Abbey House and the Tor. Such recovery of truth gives the churches responsibility for providing spiritual guidance lest people are led astray. Simple condemnation will not be respected.

During a Celtic Festival weekend in the Assembly Rooms James was asked to provide an act of Celtic worship. This was carried out drawing on the insights of the early Celtic Christian tradition and was attended by about 70 people, both churchpeople and Alternatives, and led to many requests for more, which it may be possible to provide in 1992.

The Grail Trust

During 1991 James gave up responsibility for the legal affairs of the Grail Trust and is giving up as treasurer in 1992. This followed the opening of a new retreat and conference centre at Abergenolwyn, Wales, by the Revd Jonathan Robinson, who resigned as vicar of Stoke St Gregory near Taunton in order to concentrate on this work amongst people who find little or no sustenance in the churches. Again it would seem that what will help England is respect for Celtic insights: this will bring a new unity, understanding and respect between Anglo-Saxon and Celt on the basis of equality, not dominance.

The churches

Gradually a new openness is coming to the churches as prayer, healing and study of the Christian faith is more widely accepted. This should help the churches to embrace insights which of their nature demand a far-reaching change of outlook. This is not to say that there were not those in the churches who were open to the fullness of truth when the Turnbulls first moved to Glastonbury, but they were a very small and isolated minority, most of whom had had contact with Marjorie Milne.

Following the Iona conference, the Revd Martin Reith of the Episcopal Church of Scotland paid a visit to Glastonbury and met a mixed group of churchpeople and fringe Christians, of whom there are a growing number in Glastonbury, some of whom have been influenced by St James's Piccadilly. In their exploration of some of the aspects of Celtic spirituality, of which English people are almost totally unaware, they came to the conclusion that an ecumenical act of mutual repentance and forgiveness in respect of the death of the last abbot Richard Whiting and two of his monks on the Tor is needed. Perhaps the meeting between St Augustine of Canterbury and the Welsh monks needs to be re-enacted here, together with a rerun of the Synod of Whitby, respecting the independence and value of the Celtic tradition. Priests and ministers and laypeople of many denominations could take part in what would have implications for the many Glastonbury pilgrimages, Roman, Anglican and Free Church. Maybe the Revd John Sumner could play a role in that.

> An ecumenical act of mutual repentance and forgiveness is needed for the death of the last Abbot on the Tor

The Abbey

During the summer of 1991 a number of clergy and lay readers did duty in the Abbey meeting visitors. Until such people are trained to meet the questions they raise about the whole of the Glastonbury scene (Christian, Celtic Christian and Pagan) and we learn to be honest about the shortcomings and past errors (Anglican, Roman and Free Church) this will be of little value. How long are those outside of the churches going to have to wait before the churches wake up to realize how far the people of God in England have fallen below the Christian standards of generations long ago? Nevertheless, perhaps the time is coming when there will be a springtime of the Church and the latter rain will fall before the final harvest.

The people of God in England have fallen far below the Christian standards of generations ago

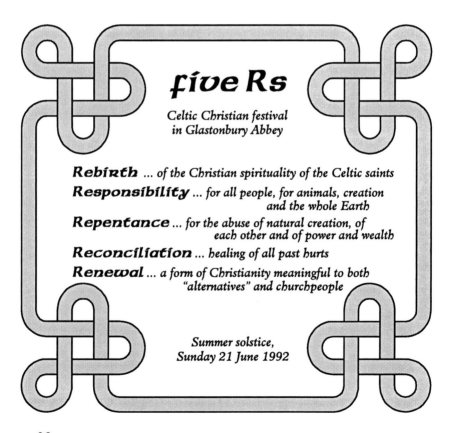

ƒíve Rs

*Celtic Christian festival
in Glastonbury Abbey*

Rebírth ... *of the Christian spirituality of the Celtic saints*

Responsíbílíty ... *for all people, for animals, creation
and the whole Earth*

Repentance ... *for the abuse of natural creation, of
each other and of power and wealth*

Reconcílíatíon ... *healing of all past hurts*

Renewal ... *a form of Christianity meaningful to both
"alternatives" and churchpeople*

*Summer solstice,
Sunday 21 June 1992*

January 1993

Ninth Glastonbury Newsletter

Growing national and world crisis

If last year's newsletter contained unpalatable truth, 1992 adds much to it which many will not like, especially C of E members, who face a major moral, financial and spiritual crisis as we cease to be the Church of the Nation, as we were in the 17th century. In every land the futility of trusting in material things becomes more evident; in Britain anxiety and insecurity increase; prosperity which depends on North Sea oil and gas and excess imports makes us militarily very vulnerable, even after the apparent end of the Cold War in which "peace" (which was no peace) was maintained by massive expenditure on nuclear weapons.

In 1992 ethnic minorities and majorities, aggrieved by past injustices, face governments and the United Nations with intractable problems and many local wars. Jews, Muslims and Hindus as well as Christians see the "great tribulation", believed to precede the Kingdom and rule of God on earth, on its way as the four horsemen of the apocalypse spread war, civil war, famine, disease and death. Such roots of conflict are to be found in our own country, even if they are played down. We tend to be a pragmatic nation.

National and local crisis

1992 in Britain revealed more centralized control, not just by Parliament but by a small number of tycoons, key figures in international finance, some corrupt, members of the cabinet and civil service, hell-bent on getting Britain into Europe. We have been serving Mammon, and the chickens are coming home to roost. The Labour Party, which lost credibility in the 1970s, cannot reach agreement with the Liberal Democrats, and this has enabled the Conservative government to pursue divisive policies as there is no effective opposition in Parliament. Inevitably, hostility of the "have nots" grows until injustice becomes so evident that there is public outcry, first about the poll tax, then the miners and now homeless people. Treatment of unemployed young people, squatters and travellers is adding to social tensions already dangerous.

Our government tries to wriggle out of the worst effects of the Treaty of Rome and the Single European Act by forcing through the Maastricht Treaty. Nevertheless many of our people are intuitively aware that we are in danger of betraying our true destiny and are selling our soul to a western European body for a doubtful mess of pottage which suits big international companies and compels us to make massive contributions to Spain, Portugal, Greece and Ireland while we renege on our responsibilities to the Commonwealth. Increasingly the Monarchy is seen by young people as irrelevant; the situation is not aided by the break-up of three royal marriages.

As Celtic culture suppressed since the time of the Roman Empire re-emerges, having continued as a spiritual undercurrent for centuries through the time of the British Empire, the scene is set for conflict which gives rise to hope that Glastonbury will become a focal point for reconciliation and national rebirth, however deep the crisis.

The church and crisis

Not surprisingly the C of E — identified with Empire, wealth and power, which has accumulated £2.7 billion of assets controlled by the Church Commissioners — has lost much of its role in the life of the nation. This has been aggravated by the rise of state education, the welfare state and the inter-faith situation. If the more obvious cause of decline in 1992 has been the barren argument over the ordination of women as priests, divisions on moral questions and finance are likely to lead to growing conflict. Apathetic outdated local churches will continue to go under, while wealthier, larger, more live ones supported by a massive church bureaucracy survive. The *Via Media*, which enabled people with conflicting views to relate to each other in the 17th century, is breaking down and, as people like Bishop Graham Leonard saw years ago, we are in for a major re-ordering of denominational structures.

> Barren argument over women's ordination led to decline in the C of E, but moral questions and finance will bring growing conflict

In spite of pain and anger giving rise to divisions, there are signs of hope. Wherever the love of Christ emerges and people respect God and each other there can be unity which cuts across all barriers. It is to that unity which Glastonbury can bear witness: people outside the churches, who may be polytheists or of other monotheistic faiths, see that Jesus does not want to sentence those who disagree with the way he is presented by his more militant followers to hellfire and damnation or to make the Church a defensive fortress, but seeks to serve us all. However much conflict between Christians at local, diocesan or national level get in the way, there are those who have eyes to see and ears to hear what makes for healing and reconciliation.

Crisis in the local church

In Glastonbury, defensive reaction is expressed when the civil authority approached St John's Church asking for railings to be erected in order to discourage travellers and local youngsters from abusing the churchyard, without making any attempt to provide for the needs of homeless people and those driven below the poverty line or unemployed. Gradually the churches are waking up, but at diocesan level the C of E is oriented to the support of a middle-class church with professional clergy costing £30,000 to support every year, which means that small rural parishes will be unable to afford paid priestly ministry. We have forgotten that 10 people tithing their income can support a full-time parson at a fraction of £30,000 — why should a small rural parish support a vast bureaucratic machine which has already taken away most of their rectories and plans to take away most if not all of their endowments? A church hierarchy which expects country people to think this is justice is living in cloud cuckoo land. Such a church is doomed, and the sooner alternative policies are worked out the better. It may be necessary for our structures to break down if they prove incapable of reform.

> Why should a small rural parish support a vast bureaucratic machine?

Through this and other upheavals the church of the future will emerge. Glastonbury, unlike Walsingham with its refusal to reconcile supporters and opponents of women's ordination, is in a unique position to play a role in reconciliation, not only between Christians but between Christians and others. To this end steps forward have been made and hopefully will continue in 1993 as it becomes evident that there are many Christians outside the churches. Nationally the C of E needs to break free of the deathwish which has gripped much of the church establishment for the whole of this century, leading to dominance of a legal, financial and administrative system that has long since outlived its usefulness. This is not "the Church against which the gates of hell cannot prevail".

A better way than violence?

It is one thing to see the way in which both Church and nation have been drifting; it is quite another to communicate with people so that we find the way through the crisis. Many nations see the answer in terms of meeting violence with violence. Not long ago we in Britain were readily supporting an unpleasant dictatorship in Kuwait against aggression from Iraq, and shortly before that we were supporting Iraq against Iran. Perhaps it is inevitable that a nation which relies on export of sophisticated arms to pay for excessive imports etc (especially from western Europe, with which we have a massive deficit) is likely to get dragged into wars; they are part of our own making. Bonhoeffer said that you cannot defeat fascist or other forms of violence with violence — was he right? Most Christians still accept, as do Muslims and others, that there is such a thing as a just war or that it is the lesser of two evils. The Alternative view in Glastonbury, which owes much to India, challenges this assumption and also challenges the patriarchal and hierarchical view which accepts that power is centralized and male-dominated; inevitably a battle is developing for our national soul.

> Most Christians still accept, as do Muslims, that there is no such thing as a just war

The Celtic festival

As reported in the eighth newsletter, the 1991 Iona conference or pilgrimage sought to come to grips with the Celtic dimension of spirituality, related to healing and to natural creation. We learnt how Celtic spirituality can help us bridge the gulf between religion and science and between sacred and secular. A further step forward was taken during 1992 when a second Celtic Festival was held in the area between the Lady Chapel and the Abbot's Kitchen in the Abbey grounds. About 150 people attended. It began by linking up circle-dancing with revolutionary thinking of unemployed young people opposed to the greed of the "haves" and convinced that moral and financial breakdown of our society is near, through corporate sin of the "haves" rather than individual sin by the "have nots". There was shared exposition of the Bible and meditation, involving openness to God and to Jesus the Christ. A bystander who asked, "Where is Jesus in all this?" received as reply, "Didn't you know he has been here all the time!" The belief of fundamentalist Christians, who see only lostness, hellfire and damnation outside of their group, was challenged by people who see God in everything and everybody (pantheism) or that everything is God (which is not true).

Not only the Celtic but the Aramaic (Arab and Assyrian) dimension played an important role in the festival; both Celtic and Aramaic Christianity accept the femininity of God.

Both Celtic and Aramaic Christianity accept God's femininity

The festival happened a week before the hierarchical male-dominated Anglican and Roman Catholic pilgrimages and was much welcomed by some churchpeople as well as Alternatives and New Age Christians. The festival raises the question of how we relate wordy church worship, which people expect to be over in an hour, to worship by people who meditate, dance and need few words. The latter respond intuitively rather than rationally and desire to worship occasionally, for much longer than an hour. At St John's Church, Preb. Patrick Riley and the Revd Liz Cross endeavour to meet this challenge with new forms of worship. As yet no follow-up to the second Celtic Festival has been planned. Most churchpeople have not yet woken up to what is happening as the shaking of the foundations of the Church continues.

Coming events and the Quest Community

During 1992 the Revd John and Mrs Alice Sumner purchased a house abutting on the Abbey with the help of the Anglican diocese and the Church Commissioners. The first two members of the Quest Community, which came into being during September 1992, are already resident in Glastonbury. Both Martin Sullivan (RC) and Kathy Butler (Anglican) are ecumenically oriented Christians not subject to vows of obedience, as are clergy. They have started work among the poor, homeless and pagans, including squatters and travellers, many of whom are Christians of a kind from whom churchpeople have much to learn. Perhaps God has fixed it so that the new community will be truly ecumenical and unitive rather than divisive, as it would be if battle for control of Glastonbury by Anglicans, Roman Catholics and Orthodox continues with lip-service to ecumenism.

As John and Alice have not yet taken up residence and the Quest Community is still going through birthpangs, and there is to be an international peace congress connected with a movement for world spiritual government during May 1993 in Glastonbury, it seems best to wait to give more time to serving the community and learning, as Martin and Kathy continue providing food and shelter for the needy. Their provision of Christmas fare in St Benedict's church hall to those in need attracted much support from both churchpeople and the wider community. True coming together for effective long-term action is likely to be slow in a community as divided as Glastonbury where many small groups operate on their own. It has started.

The masculine–feminine dilemma

Following the decision of the C of E on 11 November 1992 to ordain women to the priesthood, there will be an opportunity to include women priests in future Anglican pilgrimages to Glastonbury. Hopefully the way will eventually open up for reconciliation between advocates and opponents of ordination of women — such as Cost of Conscience, Movement for the Ordination of Women, Women Against the Ordination of Women — and those who wish to see "Women Included". The latter see Celtic spirituality as compatible with their understanding of the Christian faith. It is essential that this does not exclude Benedictine spirituality and is fully Trinitarian — not just worshipping the God-within, who replaces the God-beyond, who is dead!

> ... not just worshipping the God within, who replaces the God beyond, who is dead!

Contact with Shirley Toulson, well known author of books about Celtic spirituality, suggests it may be necessary to wait until after a conference or pilgrimage due to take place at Marygate House, Lindisfarne, in May–June 1994. This will give time for the Anglican church to begin to meet both the challenge from the proposed ordination of women and from financial crisis as Church Commissioners' funds are diverted to pay for pensions of retired clergy and to support work in poorer parts of England. Planning the agenda for the 1994 Lindisfarne conference is a priority for 1993 as we seek to face not only the masculine–feminine situation with its Celtic dimension but to link up Scotland with Wales and England on a basis of mutual respect. This can bring in the dimension of prayer and healing associated with bodies like the Guild of Health (in origin a prophetic movement associated with Percy Dearmer and Conrad Noel before the days of Fr Gilbert Shaw and Marjorie Milne).

The Guild of Health

In spite of the departure of the Methodists, the C of E was active in the 19th century. There was revival of both Catholic and Evangelical wings and massive involvement in social and educational concerns; religious orders were re-established after three centuries of virtual abeyance. The Church, however, failed to come to terms with the rise of natural science, leading to a split between the clergy and the medical profession. The Guild of Health came into being when a small number of clergy saw deep needs among both poor and sick people and sought to reverse this trend.

James became a member of the Guild council in 1982. He found that the Guild, which had played a major role nationwide until the 1960s, had been caught off-balance by development of the Christian healing ministry in parishes and congregations and then in the 1970s by charismatic renewal. The Guild needed a new sense of purpose and direction and yet, because of its insistence on the need for contemplative prayer and openness to all truth in Jesus the Christ, was still uniquely placed to make a contribution, provided it came to terms with what was happening in the spiritual life of the nation. Celtic spirituality, New Age thinking when truly spiritual, and Christ-centred awareness of the relationship between spiritual and psychic truth, between monotheism and polytheism, could help the Church move forward into the life of the nation and recover a worthwhile role in the 21st century even if some theologians and clergy oppose it.

In June 1992 the Guild undertook a pilgrimage to Oxford, and (with the help of Brian Frost, author of *Glastonbury Journey* and *The Politics of Peace*) visited centres associated with John

Wesley, with the martyrdom of Cranmer, Latimer and Ridley, with Orthodoxy, and with Cardinal Newman (a somewhat lonely but great prophetic character converted to Roman Catholicism through the ministry of the Oratory in Rome founded by St Philip Neri with the specific object of weaning back intellectuals to the Roman obedience). Oxford's spiritual riches are immense; perhaps because of our arid denominationalism and insularity many clergy and churchpeople miss out as do many of the pilgrims who come to Glastonbury. The "pilgrims" also met Bishop Stephen Verney, happily recovered and very much on the ball.

During 1993 there will be a small pilgrimage to Devon, which also has many spiritual riches of which churchpeople have lost sight. Perhaps God has raised up the New Age brand of spirituality because we have become spiritually blind. The Guild of Health stands for healing as so much more than prayer, laying-on of hands and counselling. Even if you include the ministry of deliverance and exorcism, we miss out if the image and likeness of God is not restored in people and our massive spiritual inheritance is not recovered.

We miss out if the image and likeness of God is not restored in people and our massive spiritual inheritance is not recovered

Assembly Rooms, Avalon Library, University of Avalon

If most of the high-powered performances of music and the arts, occult sciences and alternative spirituality get what to them is a disappointing response in terms of numbers when they come to Glastonbury, there can be no doubt that community plays, performed by people who live here, meet a need. There is a great deal of talent here. It appeals to men, women and children and presents a challenge to the churches. Christians are welcome provided they speak *to* and not *at* those who reject denominational Christianity. Entering this realm is not for all Christians, but without such strands the Church is impoverished, unbalanced and does not come to grips with much of the teaching of Jesus, St Paul, St John and St Peter. Proof-texts do not communicate with those who use the

Assembly Rooms, the Avalon Library or the University of Avalon, where they come to grips with issues the Church avoids and are open to hidden truth, which some condemn as occult without taking the trouble to find out what that means. When we become open to the Celtic and the feminine, new possibilities open up. It is crucial to hold fast to eternal truth as we expand our vision of God and of Christ and get to know, to love and to experience the Trinity in Unity, the masculine and feminine in God, and learn how to love our neighbour as ourselves.

> Hold fast to eternal truth as we get to know, to love and to experience the Trinity in Unity, masculine and feminine in God

On the move

The picture presented in this letter is one of the Church and the nation as seen here in Glastonbury beginning to get on the move as the battle for the soul of our country intensifies. That battle will not be won until once again the *Via Media* — the way of Christ Mediator — comes into its own. It is not enough to call Jesus Saviour and Lord. Our denominations must give up their desire to control people, as Fr Francis MacNutt indicated at a day when around 1,000 people came to Wells Cathedral last July. Perhaps the $64,000 question to ask at the beginning of 1993 is whether church establishments will hold on to power until it is wrested from them as Church foundations are shaken during a terrible time of pain and suffering.

For us at the grassroots who are not concerned with power, what matters is that we should be strong and of a good courage. It is by dying we live — if need be, through the death of denominational establishments, the City of London, Parliament and the Monarchy, as Mammon is dethroned and Jesus the Christ and God (who is the One God of Jews, Muslims, Hindus and Buddhists as well as Christians) is enthroned in its place. In this Glastonbury can play a role. In the Kingdom of God will be people at present unemployed, squatters, homeless, mentally or physically ill and starving, for we are warned that it is through great tribulation that we enter the Kingdom. Maybe there is no other way.

January 1994

Tenth Glastonbury Newsletter

Introduction

"The Church of England as it now is no power can save" is still true, but there are growing signs of renewal as more members in Glastonbury churches begin to stir. The recovery of Christian healing is developing beyond the stage of people seeking miracles, which do not always happen and can cause much distress. The arrival on the Somerset scene of the Revds David and Elsie Howell at Wellington brings in both Anglican and Baptist dimensions as well as insights from the Divine Healing Mission and the Churches' Council for Health and Healing. Fr Michael Buckley, a well known Roman Catholic priest now living near Radstock, also makes a significant contribution ecumenically. There is growing awareness of the need of many people for deep inner healing of body, mind, soul and spirit.

"Christians Together" or "Churches Together", which replaced an ineffective Council of Churches, is not yet off the ground, but the ecumenical movement is preparing to enter a new phase in which deeper theological issues come to the surface, demanding that Christians give up the power games which make unity impossible. The pace of change accelerates, pressures nationally and internationally intensify — a situation to which Turnbulls are no strangers: we lived on the borders between England and Scotland for centuries. A Turnbull from the village of Bedrule (whence James's ancestors came), who became Bishop of Glasgow and founded Glasgow University, had to steer a course between the Popes of Avignon and Rome and the Kings of Scotland (James II of Scotland was his cousin), as Rosemary discovered during a 1993 visit to Bedrule. As a student he was required to swear an oath to oppose Wyclif and Lollard "heretics" — quite alien to the Celtic tradition now happily re-emerging. Here lie roots of the rejection of episcopacy. Unity which is not unity in diversity is not unity at all.

Unity which is not unity in diversity is not unity at all

The Quest Community

It is a matter for rejoicing that the Quest Community, conceived by the Revd John and Mrs Alice Sumner in 1989, came "above ground" in Glastonbury during 1993. Early in the year an ecumenical body of trustees came into being and on Trinity Sunday a service of dedication presided over by Bishop Jim Thompson of Bath and Wells and the Revd Ian White, Methodist District Superintendent (Bristol), took place in Glastonbury Abbey. Around 300 people were present as seven men and women came forward to offer themselves, including Kathy Butler and Martin Sullivan, who after the 1992 Pilton pop festival started a daily "soup run" and provided blankets for travellers, many hungry and cold; some were children who had run away from home.

Flickers of caring by the churches

Perhaps as a consequence of this outreach, Christians have started to reach out as Alternatives have done for years, either from Marjorie Milne's house in the 1960s and 1970s and from Greenlands Farm or from the Assembly Rooms during the 1980s. Maybe the day will dawn when Glastonbury churches will give credit to Marjorie Milne, Alison Collyer, Jim Nagel, all Christians, and others including a few local residents and former squatters who cared for poor unemployed and homeless people as their predecessors in the Celtic Christian and (after centuries) Benedictine communities had done. How different is the attitude of some local churchpeople and residents who give no help where it is needed — and even bar all from entering the church and churchyard for much of the time, to stop the few who are guilty of desecration; worse still is the encouragement of vigilante violence. There are no easy solutions.

During 1993 Christians began providing regular Sunday lunches for poor and lonely people as well as making provision for Christmas and Boxing Day for those in need. This is one of a number of chinks of light differing from the darkness of Church institutions obsessed with finance and arguments about the ordination of women. The decision of those present at the AGM of the annual Anglican pilgrimage to ban women priest officiants for the foreseeable future seems as irrelevant to the 1990s as that of the circumcision party in the days of St Paul. How much wiser is the decision to respect "two integrities".

The effect of charismatic renewal

Some years ago charismatic and evangelical renewal began in a very Protestant form, worshipping God as male and moral, but it encouraged much interest in Christian healing. Most renewal is still in a Protestant form but shows signs of growth. It has brought to the surface the fear, the sense of powerlessness and the anger in men's souls. Through Kenneth McAll and others, "healing the family tree" is becoming part of Christian ministry. In some measure the "Catholic" dimension (both Anglican and Roman) brings in the feminine, even if the balance is wrong for many of us; it adds both natural and social dimensions to theology and insists on prayers for the departed.

> Healing and renewal have brought to the surface the fear, the sense of powerlessness and the anger in men's souls

Most Church structures are controlled by law and finance, based on centralized power. In a town like Glastonbury with its

Celtic as well as Anglo-Norman racial origins reinforced by incomers from other races, it does not work. Perhaps charismatic renewal can lead to the election of a local "bishop" by all the churches in the town. If the Church is to play an effective role in overcoming conflicts which stem from English class divisions *and* evils associated with the tribal divisions of Celtic society, we need a massive challenge to our top-heavy Anglican legal establishment and church bureaucracy; it has begun with "church planting". There is need for reform of episcopacy.

The C of E has created an "in-crowd" and an "out-crowd" and is saddled with a hierarchical system which lacks spiritual authority. The Celtic Church, which respected truth in science, pagan spirituality and other faiths, expanded all over Europe during the sixth to ninth centuries until suppressed by brute force. There were hundreds of bishops who exercised spiritual leadership. Today we need insights from that Church to be related to what can be learnt from Rome, Orthodoxy and from the Coptic and Nestorian churches. All this is here in Glastonbury waiting to be brought together when Christians are willing to become more open to other truth than that already held. Those whose training is based largely on Greek philosophy and Roman law find it difficult to relate to truth in modern science. Recent response to an invitation to study the writings of Susan Howatch was not encouraging. As our relationship with the Monarchy, Parliament and Synods means capacity for reform is limited, structures may have to break

Healing of
Church and
nation
links with
recovery of
Celtic insights

down. Without some form of order this can lead to chaos. There is a big task in hand for charismatic renewal if the Church is not to fail the nation.

The role of healing guilds

During 1993 Archbishop George Carey gave a remit to Bishop Morris Maddocks and the Acorn Christian Healing Trust for the next ten years; it related to the healing of Church and nation. The Council of the Guild of Health, at the root of Christian healing in England since 1904, sees this as an important part of its work and links it with recovery of Celtic insights. This work is seen as ecumenical, concerned with a prophetic dimension as well as teaching and running contemplative prayer groups.

The Churches' Fellowship for Psychical and Spiritual Studies, led by Martin Israel and Michael Perry, has a special concern for relating the Christian faith to science, spiritualism and the New Age. Barbara Bunce, former chairman of the fellowship, in her book *So Many Witnesses*, draws attention to the failure of the C of E to meet the spiritual needs of those who died in two world wars, of their comrades in arms and of their families. In particular we are suffering from the after-math of the half-million young British men killed in the battle of the Somme. In later generations many are suffering mental and spiritual as well as physical breakdown and, finding no help in the Church, turn to spiritualism or other faiths. There is need for a sound ministry of deliverance. And perhaps the support group which is coming into being for the Quest Community will help provide this and find the way for both "Catholic" and "Protestant" Christians to respect the insights of David Jenkins, the Bishop of Durham, even if they do not agree with him. None of us, not even the Bishop of Rome, knows it all — neither does the "Church here on earth".

> Mental, physical and spiritual breakdown generations later ... there is need for a sound ministry of deliverance

It has been the task of the Bath and Wells diocesan healing advisory group — the first to be established in the country, and which has an ecumenical dimension — to begin to relate the whole range of Christian insights to God, to Christ Jesus and to each other. James, who has found some progress in this direction in 1993, has also been much concerned with Family Tree Ministry. Spiritual renewal in all the churches has a long way to go; there is need for more adequate links between Christian healing, spiritual direction and soul-befriending, between Jesus and the cosmic Christ, between Christians who think they will mar their spiritual inheritance in so doing and New Agers, spiritualists and astrologers, some of whom are very wise men and women.

Further insights from the Bible in the southwest

If the "sleeping giant" (or, as some say, apostate) Church can recover the moral courage of the Celtic saints, who from the fourth to ninth centuries faced "demonic" forces then as now sweeping through the world, there are grounds for hope. It took some seventy years after the Communist revolution in Russia for this to emerge in the Soviet Union. Now we face a spiritual challenge from New Agers, spiritualists, militant Islam, from Hinduism, Buddhism and faiths associated with indigenous populations of Africa, America and Australia whose beliefs have been treated with contempt. God raised up Marcus Braybrooke and others in the West Country to stretch out a hand so that those of other faiths can see that not all Christians are raging fundamentalists even if we believe there is a specific Christian contribution still to be made. The writings of Fr Bede Griffiths are of immense value in this area and in Glastonbury there is a strong Christian presence in the Society of Friends.

> We face a spiritual challenge from those whose beliefs have been treated with contempt

There is much to learn from Quakers, who separated from the major part of the Church in England in the 17th century and suffered persecution in their stand for truth as they saw it. They have immense experience of dealing with spiritual disintegration within their movement during the 1914–18 war, when members were divided by disputes about conscientious objection to military service. Drawing on insights from George Fox, opponents learned to look at each other and see beyond the lostness and darkness in each other to the inner light and truth in Christ. Mother Teresa follows the same way as she cares for the poor dying on the streets of Calcutta.

There can be no healing of the One Church or the nation until we find that truth to unite supporters and opponents of the ordination of women as priests. Jesus warns those who cannot find that way that they neither hear nor see the Word of God. If we retire behind a defensive shell in our politics or religion we shut out the love of Christ and only see Satan in those of other faiths. In Glastonbury unemployed and homeless people — youngsters, whether locals or travellers — become alienated or antisocial. Perhaps the Society of Friends can help us rediscover the heart of true community and the Holy Grail so that the healing of the deep soul-sickness of Church and Nation will follow. Religious orders have much to teach us too. Above all we need to come to terms with the paradox of Christ.

Religious orders

During 1993 links have been explored with a number of communities, especially the Franciscans at Hilfield (Cerne Abbas), the Pilsdon Community, the Servants of the Will of God at Crawley Down in Sussex, and Benedictines both Roman and Anglican. Links also continue between Christians in Glastonbury and the Sisters of the Love of God at Fairacres, Oxford. Prayer and other support by communities is of great value for the Quest Community as it struggles to assist in the restoration of Glastonbury as a focal point for reconciliation rather than division. The support of religious orders is vital if we are to break free of the curses which stem from the Reformation period and before that, so our Church and Nation can be blessed and be a means of blessing the whole world.

The blessing and the curse

At the beginning of 1994 God is saying to us in Glastonbury: "I set before you a blessing and a curse." There will be blessing if we find a Christian form beyond "Catholic" and "Protestant", beyond national loyalties of Serb, Croat and Bosnian, beyond Israeli and Palestinian, beyond "Christian", Jew and Muslim, beyond black and white, beyond IRA and UVF, into the fullness of Christ. This demands from us in Britain humility and moral courage — strange to our reliance on force or economic imperialism based on profit, competition and injustice, which uses the police as a political weapon to suppress dissent.

> It demands from Britain humility and moral courage — strange to our reliance on economic imperialism

Barabbas should receive his just reward, but when Law and Order becomes separated from Justice, when legislation is passed by Parliament based on political slogans, people of all races, classes and cultures in Britain come under a curse. It has its roots in unspeakable events like the battle of the Somme, which has done great damage to the soul of our Church and nation. Breaking free of this curse, which leads to guerilla warfare, is primarily a matter for the recovery of the mystery which is the mystical body of Christ, the unity of the One, Holy, Catholic and Apostolic Church in which we profess to believe.

... balance between the Roman centralized form with its stress on sin and guilt, and the open, free Celtic form that emphasises the healing of deep hurts

If there is to be blessing rather than cursing there needs to be reconciliation between the Roman centralized form of Church government with its stress on sin and guilt and the teaching authority of the Church, and the open, free Celtic form with its emphasis on prophetic evangelical ministry, on healing deep hurts in people, on the communion of saints and the immortality of the soul. There is no room to explore Celtic insights further but they suggest ways and means of recovering the true meaning of episcopacy, as local oversight and as apostolic itinerant ministry free of administrative burdens. Until this happens, our Church and nation cannot recover true peace and eat of the leaves of the tree which are for the healing of the nations. God is setting before us freedom from the curse we have inherited from the past and an open door to inherit his blessing. May we in Glastonbury, in our Church and nation, choose life, as our Archbishop of Canterbury seeks to do in visiting southern Sudan at the end of 1993.

January 1995

Eleventh Glastonbury Newsletter

In writing this 11th Glastonbury newsletter the conviction has grown that recovery of Celtic insights and their relationship to our deep spiritual roots in Europe, the Middle East and Asia can enable us to enter into a richer and more complete "catholic" faith embracing a more adequate theology of Christian healing. This can help pave the way for Glastonbury to become a focal point for reconciliation in the 21st century,

A pilgrimage to the north of England during May and June 1994 gave an opportunity to meet Celtic and Anglo-Saxon saints and to explore the unity of our Three in One God and the wonder of creation. During the "Dark Ages" these saints were not slaves of history or political parties or scientific theories but — like Jesus — were free of fear of occult principalities and powers which enslave both fundamentalists with their "absolute truths" and liberals who see all truth as "relative".

This newsletter can do no more than touch on truth in a number at areas and endeavour to link them together. It aims at opening up new possibilities for those willing to launch out into the deep. The next step would seem to meet some of our Welsh friends, from whom there is much to learn; many of them have a deep understanding of the role of Glastonbury.

Rebirth of the one church in a dying world

All nations come under judgement; Britain is no exception. In days gone by it was believed that Britain with its Monarchy had replaced not just the Roman Empire and its successors but the nation state of Judah/Israel, King David and their longed-for Messiah. The British were God's chosen people of the Book (both Old and New Testaments). This belief at the heart of the 17th-century settlement between Crown, Church and Parliament, between squire and aristocrat, was implemented over the heads of landless working people and Celts. Three hundred years later things have changed: working people are educated, England can no longer destroy Irish, Scottish and Welsh culture, or appropriate Celtic wealth.

Due largely to Christian ideals, the way was prepared for the Empire to become a Commonwealth of Nations and for a new relationship with the mainland of Europe. We did not avoid judgements like the 1914–18 and 1939–45 wars or mass unemployment, but have avoided defeats like that suffered by the Highland Scots at Culloden in 1745. If, as Winston Churchill said, 1940 was "our finest hour" we were still as a nation worshipping the transcendent God of the Old Testament, repressing our feelings and keeping stiff upper lips as if impervious to suffering. Pacifists and shell-shocked men were treated as cowards and weaklings, and we were unaware of the damage being done to our national soul. For all this and much more, Church and nation in Britain come under judgement.

Honest to God gave rise first to charismatic renewal, then to a deeper and more far-reaching spiritual renewal now on its way

After 1945 we in Britain faced the twilight of our national "god" with our division of people into goodies and baddies. We had an inadequate hold on a fully Trinitarian faith. There came a new awareness of God-within as a counter to our "dualism". John Robinson wrote *Honest to God*; reaction to it gave rise, first to charismatic renewal, then to a deeper and more far-reaching spiritual renewal now on its way. [In the wake of the sacking of two priests by their bishops in 1994, much trumpeted by the newspapers,] maybe the question to ask is whether the C of E is guilty of hypocrisy and double standards; great care needs to be taken to guard against abuse of power, if clergy freehold is to be abolished. Maybe the time is coming ripe for a recovery of a fully Trinitarian faith embracing long-lost Celtic areas of truth.

Through conflict to renewal

Following the ministry of the late Marjorie Milne and, before her, Fr Gilbert Shaw, the nature of Celtic spirituality is gradually re-emerging in Glastonbury as elsewhere. It has much in common with Eastern "Orthodox" belief and with Coptic and Nestorian traditions. The heart of ancient Celtic faith and science (with which modern scientists and theologians are only now *beginning* to catch up) was learnt and handed down by oral tradition, as befitted people who lived close to nature and were craftsmen who distrusted "truth" in the written word (as believed by the Mediterranean peoples of two thousand years ago). Their institutions were communities rather than hierarchical structures with their "them" and "us". At their best they were not into power and money games, associated with Roman and Norman traditions with their passion for domination of subject nations and their zeal for conversion to a superior (?) faith. The Celts, however, were tribal without any form of central organization; inevitably they lost out to the Romans.

> Celtic spirituality has much in common with Eastern Orthodox belief and with Coptic and Nestorian traditions

In England we have, since the Reformation, dealt with conflict which stems from our mixture of nations and tribes, by compromise. As can be seen in Scotland and Ireland, Celts do not compromise, but may be open to reconciliation of opposites held together by entering into the mystery of the paradox of Cross and Resurrection. No national church is perfect, and because of this — as Jesus warned — occasions of stumbling will come. He added: "Woe to those through whom they come." In 1994 we might add: "whether they are members of the Royal Family, members of Parliament, bishops, senior churchmen, or ordinary people like you and me who find ourselves victimized by distortions of truth, or by an Establishment which supports the strong against the weak". Inevitably, all our institutions are under attack as hidden truth is brought to light accompanied by lies, accusations and counteraccusations within Church and nation and on the international scene. Not surprisingly, people desert political parties and denominational structures in droves; the cry goes up to heaven that leaders are unfair, as they force their policies through, and find that cover-up to avoid scandal becomes more difficult. Inevitably protests against injustice grow in number and scope, which leads to social disintegration and, in many countries, to civil war. A new form of leadership is needed.

Leadership and the crisis of authority

There is a big difference between the Celtic way and the Roman and Norman way of leadership. In the 6th-century Celtic church the custom was to look for guidance to holy men and hermits: not to "boss" figures who try to resolve tensions by imposing decisions made by those in power. It would seem that we need to relive the conflict between Celtic and Anglo-Roman authority of the seventh and eighth centuries before healing of our Church and nation can come. Deep spiritual renewal and grassroots revival means that the power of divisive party theologies and financial control by the Church Commissioners and by diocesan structures needs to be broken, so that the "Church Establishment" can become subject to the authority of Christ. The need for fairness and justice will intensify as our financial crisis deepens, and roots of division between traditionalists and their liberal opponents emerge.

Unity comes when we look for guidance to saints who understand the length, breadth, depth and height of the universe; bishops and church leaders need to be patient and humble, filled with the love of Christ, of God and of people. They become soul-friends rather than rich overloads. Here lies hope of bridging the gulf between Episcopalian and Presbyterian, justice for our smaller and less prosperous congregations and for the homeless and the poor: of this the C of E "Establishment" needs to take note.

An example of the destructive tendencies growing in our country is to be seen in London, where £1 million was spent on cleaning the fabric of a church whilst homeless people starved and even died on its doorstep. Iron railings were erected to keep them out of the shelter the church had provided; that is a recipe for anarchy and destruction. No wonder millions give up worship and turn to paganism, as Christians argue about doctrines as "absolute moral truths" but fail to care for the poor as local and international conflicts are whipped up by winds of change sweeping the world. Our dying nation is to be seen when 17½ percent VAT is added to the price of fuel, workers are made redundant as money pours into the pockets of bosses in electricity, gas and water industries. Our continent is dying as fraud mounts in a Europe of centralized power, stemming from the Treaty of Rome, backed by France, Germany and the Vatican. Britain is dying when the executive usurps the role of Parliament and prepares to hand over our national sovereignty in disregard of our history. The end of the 20th century is not easy for those in power in Church and State.

As the rate of change accelerates, pressures mount. More and more half-baked legislation is passed by Parliament to the despair of people with first-hand experience; party political dogma resorts to tyranny to preserve Law and Order; Parliament is brought into disrepute. The disadvantaged cry to heaven, as in 1994 a grassroots upsurge grows, which may help us avert disaster. We need renewal deeper than that which took place in the fifteenth to seventeenth centuries before and after the tyranny of Henry VIII. Such a spiritual renewal in the sixth to tenth centuries led to the glory of God being spread abroad through the Celtic Church, whose members were set on fire with the love of God. Maybe this depth of renewal can be recovered now to aid rebirth of our British Church and nation. In this, Glastonbury and the Quest Community have a part to play if the churches and Alternatives become involved together, as happened in Britain many centuries ago.

> As change accelerates, we need deep renewal ... the glory of God spreading abroad

The Quest Community and local churches

The Quest Community received much publicity when three men and four women were admitted to membership of the "core group" during June 1993. From the outset members were flung into action before they had learnt to be a community, as a result of the needs of travellers and homeless people who spread the word around, and also through the publicity which at times engulfs Glastonbury. Many who come here are alienated from their families or have been losers in the search for jobs, at a time when massive unemployment has been deliberately created by a government increasingly out of touch with ordinary people and blind to genuine needs, and forces through unworkable and unjust laws like the Criminal Justice Bill. Inevitably many people are very angry, even if a growing number of Christians and others seek to defuse the situation.

A government increasingly blind to genuine needs forces through unjust laws like the Criminal Justice Bill

There is much fear abroad of travellers and the poor. Some is directed at Alternatives who resort to belief in spirits, magic, the psychic dimension and reincarnation (the last *not* ruled out by early Christians). Some members of churches have begun to explore "family tree ministry" as an extension to a ministry of prayer and Christian healing which began some years ago. Others have begun to face up to the extent to which materialism has eroded Christian credibility. Others still try to take the mote out of the eyes of those outside the Church before we have removed the beam from our own. As some Christians respond to the challenge, others feel threatened, ignore what is happening, or revert to outdated theological power games in pursuit of what is believed to be the truth. A different way of life is being put before us by the Quest Community whose members seek to serve the poor and relate to those outside of the churches as friends. Christians who seek mediation are cooperating; extremists and fundamentalists who think they have all the answers are not.

Grounds for hope lie in recovery of a spirituality with profound belief in the One God who relates to the whole of life, as we explore the Celtic and Indian dimensions of spirituality. A 1994 visit to Glastonbury by Brother Martin, from Fr Bede Griffiths' ashram in India, evoked a good response from people who find our denominational theologies to be barriers to the truth. Groundwork aimed at seeking a soundly based Celtic spirituality was laid with a pilgrimage to the north of England to learn from the Celtic saints. There is need to hold fast to the narrow way of Cross and Resurrection if we are not to be swept away by syncretism, which would undermine Christian witness in Glastonbury.

Celtic witness from the north

Up to twenty-eight of us from Scotland, Wales and various parts of England from a variety of denominations, including a goodly number of members of the Guild of Health council, visited Whitby, Lastingham, Durham, Jarrow and Lindisfarne; a few of us went to Lichfield Cathedral. Thanks to the sisters of Order of the Holy Paraclete at Whitby, to the head verger at Durham Cathedral (a Somerset man), to Revd John Pritchard, warden of St John's College Durham (formerly of Somerset), to Revd Paul Baker of St Paul's Jarrow, to the warden of the Bede Museum, to Revd Kate Tristram and Canon David Adam of Lindisfarne, new dimensions opened up to us. We became aware of a spiritual base which transcended race, class, sex, and creed, whilst holding fast to the heart of Christian belief after suffering defeat and humiliation at the hands of enemies. We learnt that if we are sufficiently rooted and grounded in the truth there is no need to fear — let alone condemn or curse — those who oppress us.

The Celtic saints loved and forgave their enemies, and this example was followed by early Anglo-Saxon saints: St Hilda, St Chad, St Cedd, St Cuthbert and others who learnt of Celtic tradition from St Aidan and other

> The Celtic saints loved and forgave their enemies ... they were able to blend together spiritualities

Celts from Iona and Melrose, as well as Lindisfarne. They were able to blend together Celtic, Anglo-Saxon and Roman spirituality, whilst St Augustine of Canterbury (and Augustine of Hippo), St Wilfrid, St Boniface and those who hold to one-sided "absolute truths" imposed by hierarchical elites could not. There is a difference between Romanism and being "catholic", as many Roman Catholics (amongst whom are many saints) are aware.

The north bears witness that the term "catholic" should include the Celtic dimension. This does not mean a sloppy liberal theology in which alleged scientific reasons are found to condone every kind of evil, but by living out truth and following a way of life so patently holy, that it can be respected by pagans and Alternatives as well as churchpeople. It calls for the rebirth of the One Church in which through patience, humility and love we can relate to Alternatives and to "fundamentalists" of all faiths, Jewish, Christian, and Muslim, and to nationalist zealots just as Terry Waite did when a prisoner in Beirut, and Jesus did long before that.

> It does not mean a sloppy liberal theology in which alleged scientific reasons are found to condone every kind of evil

The north of England bears witness to a faith like this; it transcends the rich–poor divide; it can help the C of E in southern England break free of a system which suits rich parishes and cathedrals, and is applied willy-nilly to smaller and less prosperous parishes required to support expensive clergy, as the church follows the state in establishing an over-centralized bureaucracy. This administrative system creates an "in-crowd" and an "out-crowd", whether in town or country, because it has little sense of community, and makes for political and church leadership which becomes tyrannical. The "in-crowd" sees nothing wrong with it, but it will break down, and it needs to be challenged. Perhaps Glastonbury will provide a way through, as the Celtic and Indian dimensions are recovered.

To those who have grown up since the 19th-century divide between religion and science, who accept denominational or party theology to prove their own point of view or to lambast their opponents, the belief that all knowledge is interrelated, and that "the Lord our God is one Lord", is not truly accepted. The day, however, when sciences are empirical, scientists ignore spiritual truth, and clergy ignore science, is going: partly through Susan Howatch's gift of £1m to Cambridge University.

Modern science is now moving in the direction of Celtic spirituality (like that of the Old Testament) where there is only one God: Earth, Paradise and Heaven, science, politics and religion, are all part of one order, embracing natural creation, spiritual and celestial worlds, inhabited by gods, spirits, angels, archangels, principalities and powers, as well as human beings. In Celtic spirituality Mary — the feminine — has a role in her own right, not subservient to the male patriarchal view of religion.

> Modern science is moving in the direction of Celtic spirituality, where there is only one God

As the mystery of the Trinity in Unity — with its male and female dimensions — opens up, so we can know more of the wonder of the One God of all creation, visible and invisible, making for growth in love of God and of our neighbour as ourselves. Perhaps if we follow this route, theology can once again become "Queen of Sciences".

As we follow in the footsteps of Mary, and of Jesus to whom Mary points, we become more whole, holy people made in the image and likeness of God — sons of men — more like the cosmic Christ of creation. In the Celtic tradition this also means following the way of John the beloved disciple, with dreams and visions of the seer or contemplative who attains to purity of heart and deep inner serenity. Early Celtic Christians found his approach more in line with their pre-Christian tradition.

Vision for the future

1994 has opened up new dimensions in Glastonbury. A new revelation of God is on its way with implications for Monarchy, Church and state. The time when the term "catholic" can be limited to the Roman or Anglo-Catholic view of truth has gone: we are moving into one world not just of European nations, nor of the five continents, but of natural powers, angels and archangels (holy and not-so-holy), spirits and elemental spirits (earth, air, fire and water), connected with the cherubim and seraphim. Cherubim are connected with earth and water, with the beast in men, with law and forgiveness; seraphim with wind and fire, with the prophetic spirit and with the dragon.

True catholicism includes Orthodox and Celtic dimensions and is centred on the Trinity-in-Unity, way beyond the earthbound spirituality of contemporary Britain. Jesus certainly embraced all these dimensions, and to follow Him in this way enabled Celtic saints to overcome the fear with which we face the supernatural, and grow in the courage to overcome hardship and danger in alien cultures ruled over by cruel dictators.

As a new and richer revelation of truth comes, Mary and Christ pave the way for a new heaven and a new earth, to help us face the time when our national spiritual bankruptcy will be exposed: even more than at Dunkirk. To meet the situation we need to find the way to love our enemies so that our Christian faith enables us to relate creatively to hardline Jewish, Christian and Muslim fundamentalists, who insist they alone have the truth. To the archangels Gabriel, Raphael and Michael, beloved of Orthodoxy, we need to add Phanuel or Uriel, the archangel of revelation, who helps to make the faith once delivered to the saints full and complete, as it was in the early Church.

Love our enemies so that our Christian faith enables us to relate creatively to hardline Jewish, Christian and Muslim fundamentalists

The Celtic dimension goes beyond ancient sciences such as astrology and the belief of the Magi, and relates religion to natural science. I believe that, as at the time of St Aidan and St Hilda, it can once more include the law of Rome, and the philosophy of Greece. It develops our understanding of British myths as well as Teutonic and Mediterranean myths already taught in our schools. We are taken beyond Toronto Blessings connected with the cherubim (and if we are not careful, with right-wing politics and the beast); and beyond the social gospel connected to the seraphim (which veers towards left-wing politics, and the dragon). The Celtic dimension brings cherubim and seraphim together and relates the manhood of Jesus to the divinity of the cosmic Christ of creation; this means creation and redemption become opposite sides of the same coin, thus completing the paradox.

This is the narrow way, not of obeying puritanical laws and rules, but of holding fast to Christ Jesus and the Spirit of the living God, preparing through suffering to see and to enter the Kingdom of God. A way of hope is developing here in Glastonbury — let there be no doubt about that. It is in tune with the biblical revelation, though we may need to look at the Bible in a new light, which is the light of Christ.

May you and I go forward to walk in the way that the Lord God sets before us, and become open and vulnerable, even if we get hurt, as we seek to obey the will of our Heavenly Father revealed through His Son, Jesus Christ.

January 1996

Twelfth Glastonbury Newsletter

During 1995 it has been possible to learn more of the spiritual inheritance in our beloved land. Visits to Wales and Lindisfarne opened up more awareness of Celtic and Anglo-Saxon saints; they are still alive. They challenge contemporary belief in "subsidiarity" in Church and state as advocated by the Turnbull Commission and the Treaty of Rome. The doctrine of "subsidiarity" has its roots in the Roman Empire. The British Crown, Parliament, the EEC, the General Synod of the C of E and the Papacy have authority only insofar as they are under the authority of God. Teaching and Law are not above Prophecy and Revelation.

A major rediscovery this year was a 13th-century fragment of St Patrick's Charter, belonging to nearby St Nicholas Church, West Pennard. It refers to St Benignus (or Beonna) and twelve monks, and roots and grounds our ancient spiritual tradition with the remains of the saint transferred from nearby Meare in 1091. The dedication of the church built at that time was changed to St Benedict in the 17th century, during the time of witchcraft scares when "Protestants" were in control, and laws were passed through fear of abuse of power by Rome to ban Roman Catholics from the throne of England.

This ancient tradition related our Christian faith in Britain to St John, to natural creation, to Church and State, and to our Celtic ancestors with their pagan and Old Testament roots. Sadly this faith, undermined by Norman invasion and domination by Rome, became urban and Mammon-oriented, patronizing and worse to the poor and to simple country folk; we became rooted in Empire, not in God.

This newsletter seeks to rediscover a spiritual base for unity between all the churches in Britain on the basis of mutual respect, not on compulsion or "subsidiarity", but on humility, patience and love. The opportunity has now come for past errors to be put right within and beyond Glastonbury if the will is there.

> Opportunity has now come for past errors to be put right within and beyond Glastonbury

State of the Church of England

The state of the nation is becoming so obvious it needs no comment. Sadly, as the battle for the soul of the nation hots up, churches become weaker; where there is renewal as there is in bodies like "Forward in Faith", in Evangelical or charismatic Christianity into "Toronto Blessings", and in hardline Catholic and Protestant morality, we become more divided; woolly liberals do not help. When (as the Nine O'clock Service bears witness) re-emerging creation and Celtic spirituality is not soundly based it leads to disaster. The C of E is like a woman in travail who does not have the strength to bring to the birth a body of people who transcend denominational boundaries and conflicting theologies, and fails to be credible to many of her own members, let alone those of other faiths and none.

On the other hand we are recovering the heart of the Celtic Christian and Old Testament basis of our faith, and this enables us to see truth in Christ Jesus and Mary in a new light. It will lead to attempts to modify our structures; life will become very uncomfortable for church hierarchies, especially in the Anglican and Roman traditions. Maybe Jonathan Sacks, our Chief Rabbi, can help if his book *Faith in the Future* is read by Christians willing to explore our Jewish roots and Jewish awareness of what it is to be members of one body of people.

Perhaps our contemporary dilemma stems from

principalities and powers and elemental spirits which are not brought under the authority of Christ. This results in unconscious and unhealthy fear of "occult powers" and disregard of abuse of power within the Church. Indian spirituality has much to contribute. Bede Griffiths reminds us that not only powers associated with earth, air, fire and water need to be taken into account but also forces associated with electricity, gravity and magnetism. The heart of Indian spirituality relates natural science to religion, sacred to secular, and helps Church hierarchies and grassroots avoid getting caught up in the power game. Perhaps the whole Church in England has to be purified through such suffering if we are to make an effective contribution to science politics and morality again. The day for that has not yet come.

> The heart of Indian spirituality relates science to religion, sacred to secular, and avoids getting caught up in the power game

Dealing with the crisis within church structures

The C of E has dealt with our current crisis in central structures by establishing the Turnbull Commission (nothing to do with the author of this newsletter!). The brief given to the commission, as with the commission set up to prepare the way for synodical government in 1964, is seriously flawed. Our present diocesan structures are not brought into question as they were by the Paul Report of the early 1960s. They are still based on large areas of land under legal control, not on communities with personal spiritual leadership that encourages the prophetic dimension. Inevitably the local parish or congregation is constricted by demand for conformity to out-of-touch centralized power backed up by a huge bureaucracy acting in the name of the bishop — personal contact gets lost; our sense of being members of one body is destroyed.

It follows that attempts made to abolish clergy freehold are frustrated; we forget that curates (and priests in charge) are treated differently from those with a freehold and are sometimes victims of injustice; clergy with permission to officiate are not even given permission to vote in parishes where they reside or worship. As yet opposition to the Common Fund by the grassroots has scarcely begun. At best the Turnbull Commission is a first step at a time when finance and theology are likely to tear asunder the parochial and diocesan structure of the C of E. We still prefer the illusion of "safety" in the ancient Roman pattern to recovery of the risk-taking Celtic dimension with its insistence that all generations, past, present and future — earth, paradise and heaven — are part of one order; only when hierarchy and synod surrender desire for control can we come to know and love the Holy Trinity, as the Church breaks free of the limitations of the rational Enlightenment and materialism and becomes one body of people. Reform needs to begin at the top but will not be easy.

With true freedom we can become part of a Church that is not turned in defensively on itself, but able to reach out to every area of life. Evangelism with its excessive individualism becomes subject to authority as we learn to render to Caesar — to earthly authority in Church and State — what is Caesar's, and to God what belongs to God; no longer does Mammon rule in the Church. Collapse is avoided as renewal comes based on the fullness of Christ, on paradox, not on partial truth which divides us into "Catholic" and "Protestant".

During the last thirty years there has been an increase in non-stipendiary ministry, but our structures, like old bottles, are still far too inflexible. Many smaller and less prosperous parishes, especially in the country, have been and are being milked of funds, multi-parish linkups force clergy to relate to more and more congregations; administrative tasks multiply to the detriment of the "cure of souls" — signs of a dying Church. Little thought is being given to establishing small dioceses where there is better contact between bishop and people, as in the early Church, as we restore a truly apostolic ministry and reduce the number of expensive, fully stipendiary clergy. Able laity despair of the C of E, except where an indigenous ministry of lay pastors, teachers and evangelists develops so that the body can begin to become alive. Not all the blame for disunity can be laid at the door of the community churches or of the Church

Establish small dioceses for better contact between bishop and people, as in the early Church

Establishment. First we need to take the beam out of our own eye whoever we are.

Meeting the challenge in Glastonbury

James and Rosemary, with experience in small rural and unfashionable parishes, moved to Glastonbury in 1980. We had the benefit of contact from the 1960s with Roman Catholics who had a genuine ecumenical concern, with people like Anna Harper from Brighton trying to help youngsters addicted to heroin on her own, with Marjorie Milne of Glastonbury who saw the value of Celtic spirituality for those outside as well as within the churches, with Brian Frost — author of *Glastonbury Journey* and *The Politics of Peace*, then director of the Churches' Council for Health and Healing — and with many others: some bishops, some members of religious orders.

With its pagan as well as Christian roots which attract people from far and wide, Glastonbury has possibilities for reconciliation in which Christians who accept truth in other faiths can play a role. Fear of this in the churches is deep; many, both "Catholics" and "Protestants", feel threatened.

Pagan as well as Christian roots draw people to Glastonbury from far and wide: Christians who accept truth in other faiths have a role in reconciliation

Like Britain, Glastonbury is a divided society. By 1980 Mrs Alison Collyer at Greenlands Farm was caring for travellers and homeless people, some local-born and bred. This attracted opposition and by 1987 Greenlands was forced to close its doors through legal action and lack of finance. Whether of local origin or "travellers", disturbed young people may steal and cause problems; some become dirty — especially if denied facilities to wash. Those whose family life has broken up are homeless or addicted to alcohol or drugs become a threat to those addicted to materialism. Vigilantes sought and still seek to drive away some who seek asylum here; opposition intensifies until churchpeople and Alternatives who want to help are threatened. Places where the poor can find shelter are barred not only in Glastonbury. Awareness that all is not well has spread; a committee based on County Hall in Taunton is bringing together people from various parts of Somerset to consider a response more positive than eviction of harassed people with the help of riot police. Democracy is at work even if as yet ineffective.

Local churches

"Christians Together" in Glastonbury has become aware that churches and community have drifted far apart. Worship in church and pilgrimages to Glastonbury — whether Roman or Anglican or more recently evangelical charismatic — have made little impact on the life of the town. Two and a half years ago the Quest Community came into being here and has begun to explore with the churches and some Alternatives how we can break free of past quarrels. It is abundantly clear that divided sections of the One Church with a sense of denominational or party superiority, who expect others to come round to their point of view, provide no basis for reconciliation. Those who develop a ministry of Christian healing and are uncharitable to members of the National Federation of Spiritual Healers [which has shopfront premises in the Market Place] have little respect from Alternatives or from the medical profession. There are positive signs; more people see hope in Jesus as a renewed Church begins to reconcile the irreconcilable.

> Those with a sense of superiority, who expect others to come round to their point of view, provide no basis for reconciliation

Turnbull commitments

Due to age and other commitments James has given up involvement with the Assembly Rooms, Children's World (a local charity) and the Grail Trust. He continues helping out in parishes around and remains ecumenical member of the Bath and Wells diocesan healing advisory group, and the Guild of Health council. He has joined the Thomas Merton Society and the Somerset county review panel for policy towards traveller eviction, and continues to plan pilgrimages and maintain contacts in various parts of England, Scotland, Wales and Ireland. Rosemary has given up much of her Mothers' Union work, has ceased to stand for St Benedict's PCC and playing the piano for Prayer and Praise at St John's Church (which now takes place twice a month as "Toronto Blessings" attract as many as 150 people). Since August she has stood in for the organist at St Benedict's Church, who has been seriously ill.

Quest seeks to back up churches in caring for poor people and in welcoming pilgrims to Glastonbury

Both Rosemary and James continue with various ecumenical prayer groups and have become companions and "godparents" of the Quest Community, which has an ecumenical body of trustees. Among other activities the Quest Community seeks to back the churches in caring for poor people and welcoming pilgrims and visitors to Glastonbury, and publishes a periodical called *Glastonbury Thorn*. The stand by Christians in the town has begun to register with the local council. [Quest has been given use of the recently refurbished medieval almshouses next to St Margaret's Chapel, off Magdalene Street.]

Pilgrims

Following our mini-pilgrimage to the north of England in 1994 James and Rosemary took part in a retreat or conference at Lindisfarne in October–November 1995 led by the Community of Aidan and Hilda. This community has roots in East Anglia and seeks the restoration of Celtic spirituality through retreats, encouraging soul-friends, teaching, writing, new liturgy and prayer. The warden is Ray Simpson; the community has an ecumenical body of trustees, both Scots and English. It has arrived at conclusions which have much in common with those pioneered by Marjorie Milne with her Scottish, Indian, Welsh and English roots.

Rosemary and James also spent ten days in 1995 making a preliminary visit to Wales to plan another mini-pilgrimage for June 1996. The impression gained is that the Welsh Church, since disestablishment (and disendowment) in 1912, has learnt from Welsh saints and the Welsh national tradition a humility which our English Establishment and renewal groups lack; maybe we English Christians have yet to adjust to loss of Empire and to learn that only the humble are exalted.

Pilgrimages to Glastonbury

The 1995 West of England Pilgrimage, now representing only the opponents of the ordination of women in its policy, duly took place. The decision was taken at the September AGM to drop local Anglican bishops from their supportive role and to rename this annual event the "Glastonbury Pilgrimage". This title is a nonsense as the organizers know little or nothing of Glastonbury.

Evangelical charismatics connected with "Hearts on Fire" celebrated a substantial gathering in the Abbey during July, but many of them are refusing to cooperate with other Christians who seek to relate to pagans and those of other faiths. Not only the Vatican and opponents of women's ordination are hardline. It is perhaps significant that Michael Eavis, who established the massive annual "pilgrimage" at nearby Worthy Farm, Pilton [the pop festival that began in 1971], hopes to stage a festival of classical music in Glastonbury Abbey in 1996. These trends point to the future of the Christian Church as bleak without recovery of the Celtic dimension at its best.

Perhaps the most important local pilgrimage of 1995 was a small gathering of "Christians Together in Glastonbury" who spent a day in December at the Friends Meeting House in Street. This gathering included Methodists, Anglicans, URC *and* a strong contingent from the local evangelical charismatic Community Church. A representative from each church led worship for an hour; there was the beginning of repentance and forgiveness which could lead to prayer and outreach to Roman Catholics, Orthodox, Quakers and others as awareness of the hurts which Christians have inflicted on each other over the centuries makes for a far-reaching change of heart here in Glastonbury.

> Awareness of the hurts Christians have inflicted on each other over the centuries makes for far-reaching change of heart in Glastonbury

We can take heart that 1995 saw an Orthodox presence in Glastonbury with roots in the Coptic Church of Egypt and the desert fathers. There are also local Christians into the mystical Aramaic dimension, which believes in God as Father-Mother and has an understanding of creation different from orthodox belief. They have much in common with saints like Mother Julian of Norwich and the Franciscan tradition. When all give up the desire to compel others to conform to their vision of Christ, the way may emerge to redeem the murkier parts of our past in Glastonbury and transcend denominational barriers. Cooperation has begun with plans for the purchase of a centre for ecumenical Christian outreach to the community.

The wider scene

1994 and 1995 have shown the Turnbulls that St Aidan, St Hilda, St Cedd, St Chad, St Cuthbert and a host of Celtic and Saxon saints provide a spirituality which can transcend denominational and national barriers. Roots of this are to be found locally. This emerged when the Mid-Somerset Group of the National Association of Decorative and Fine Arts presented its report based on more than two years' work connected with St Nicholas' Church, West Pennard, three miles from Glastonbury. The report referred to the Charter of St Patrick, which mentions St Benignus (or Beonna) and other saints at the heart of tradition in the medieval Abbey and makes room for the Celtic dimension. Perhaps the charter was connected with the Franciscan renewal in the 13th century. There is a fragment of 13th-century origin which belongs to West Pennard parish church and tells of twelve saints in addition to St Beonna who were in the same area of spirituality as the Celtic and Saxon saints of Scotland and of the northeast, with roots in desert and Irish spirituality.

The strand preserves truth which St Augustine, St Wilfrid, St Boniface and possibly St Dunstan (whose spirituality was corrupted by aggression and nationalism) did not honour. It was denied both by the "Catholic" Inquisition and by the "Protestant" stand for truth and was based on humility and holiness, not on Church–State alliances which prevent us from becoming one body. It is here that the Turnbull Commission fails because it is based on centralized power, not on the obedience of faith as lived out by humble Celtic bishops with the belief in One God and that all truth relating to the One God is interwoven. This strand links faith with science, with natural as well as spiritual powers, with mathematics and history, the arts and morals. The way opens up for an end to the separation between sacred and secular which plagues an urban-based power-oriented church. 1997 will give a great opportunity to change all this.

Pilgrimage from Rome to Ireland via Britain

There is to be a major pilgrimage starting in Rome passing through Canterbury, the Midlands and the north of England, to Wales and Scotland in 1997. A spur is planned to start in Cornwall to pass through Devon and Somerset, including Crediton and Glastonbury, on the way to Aust and St David's. It gives an opportunity to heal the damage caused by St Wilfrid in 664 at the Synod of Whitby and even earlier damage caused to relationships between Christians when St Augustine met the Welsh bishops in 602. If this damage is healed, Christians will respect those of other denominations, including those who do not accept episcopacy in its present form. This is very difficult for many Anglicans, especially those into power games. Perhaps that is why a pilgrimage to Ireland with the decision to end at Derry (Londonderry) is so important as a signal that Rome and England both seek to act, like Jesus, as servants of the people of God, not masters.

... a signal that both Rome and England seek to act, like Jesus, as servants, not masters

The pilgrimage gives us in the southwest an opportunity to explore not only St Augustine, St Boniface and St Dunstan but Celtic saints, both Cornish and Welsh, as well as Our Lady, St Patrick, St Bridget, St David, and St Gildas. To this we can add St Beonna and his twelve monks as well as St Joseph of Arimathea and St Aristobulus, who are part of our ancient roots in Celtic Christianity and those in other faiths who walk humbly with the Three-in-One God. Members of the Quest Community sought to explore these roots at their centre in the Coracle, their "bender" at the 1995 Pilton pop festival.

Perhaps in this pilgrimage lies hope for a divided Church

and a divided nation as the 20th century draws to a close. We in Britain, and England in particular, need to adapt to loss of power and status in the world, which stems from Empire and does not have spiritual roots in the One God who creates and redeems not only the whole of mankind, but the whole creation. There are spiritual riches like treasure buried in a field in Glastonbury. Perhaps we will rediscover them, as we reconsider our belief in the light of Peter, Paul, Matthew and John — integrating the pastoral, evangelistic, teaching and prophetic views of truth in Christ, with respect for all that is of God in other faiths.

> There are spiritual riches like treasure buried in a field in Glastonbury

January 1997

Thirteenth (and last?) Glastonbury Newsletter

Introduction

1996 has been a year of challenge to the Turnbulls. By the end of the year it was apparent that some interests must be given up; it becomes increasingly difficult to remain in touch with the manifold spiritual and psychic strands which affect this unusual place with its potential for conflict as well as for reconciliation. Hopefully *Glastonbury Thorn*, the new magazine which informs about the difficult work undertaken by the Quest Community, will help the Church in England take note of what is happening here as the millennium approaches.

Perhaps the first need for many Christians today is to follow the advice of the late Bishop John Robinson in *Honest to God*: to hold fast to Christ and for everything else to be uncommitted. The biography of Robert Runcie by Howard Carpenter suggests that he follows that route; others like George Carey, our present archbishop, may look more to Jesus, the author and perfecter of our faith. Fullness of the catholic faith, as Cardinal Hume has said, demands attentive listening. To those of us reared in both the Catholic and Protestant traditions with inputs from Orthodoxy and from other faiths, this does not mean just listening to a hierarchy which expects to be obeyed or to powerful charismatic figures who seek to impose theological insights and moral "absolutes" on us all. Perhaps the bishop who admits he does not understand the present Archbishop of Canterbury, let alone those in more far-reaching disagreement with his theological position, would benefit from listening to St James, who presided over the first Council of Jerusalem in AD49. We need to sift what purports to be truth, in the light of the person of Christ Jesus, as we come to terms with the masculine and the feminine in God and in our own personalities, as we explore the riches of Celtic and creation spirituality at its best. Here we find a catholicity purged of elements which give rise to abuse of power by Church and State in Britain and on the continent of Europe.

In Britain we see both strengths and weaknesses in people; profoundly spiritual men and women "saints" are not infallible. We can grow to accept that "fundamentals" of the faith, whether Catholic or Protestant, may help prepare the way for the coming of the Holy Spirit as John the Baptist prepared the way for the coming of the Messiah. We can include Alternative insights into truth even if more "fundamentalist" members of the church find this difficult. In the New Testament we are reminded that the least in the Kingdom of God is greater than John.

Perhaps Prince Charles, who insists on relating his Christian faith to other religions as a result of the influence of Laurens van der Post, can help our country find a spiritual basis for peace which is true peace, and Glastonbury — the British Jerusalem — can play a role which Jerusalem in the Holy Land, little nearer to peace now than two thousand years ago when Jesus the Christ walked along its streets including the Via Dolorosa, cannot do. At present our Church is in a muddle and our political leadership panders to the blind mouths of which the poet Milton complained in the 17th century. A new vision for the people of Britain is needed for the millennium. There is need for far-reaching change.

> Perhaps Glastonbury can play a role which Jerusalem, little nearer to peace now than in Jesus' time, cannot do

138

Local developments

Gradually a measure of new life has come to Glastonbury churches. Plans are currently being made for Glastonbury to act as host to 50 pilgrims during May who, starting from Penzance, intend to commemorate the 1400th anniversary of the arrival in England of St Augustine from Rome and the death of St Columba on Iona. They will join a larger body at Aust near Bristol on the way to Wales and Derry (Londonderry) in Northern Ireland, where some five hundred pilgrims are due to assemble. Some are due to start in Rome and travel through Italy and France to Britain, but the main pilgrimage will start in Canterbury and follow various routes through England, Scotland and Wales to Ireland. There will be an opportunity for some members of other faiths to meet pilgrims who come here, though the pilgrimage is basically an ecumenical Christian venture. In Glastonbury it has already brought representatives from the Orthodox, Roman Catholic and strongly evangelical Community Church together with those in Anglican and Free Church traditions. That is progress.

Glastonbury Abbey is host to the more traditional Anglican pilgrimage, now firmly in the hands of the opponents of the ordination of women, and to the Roman Catholic pilgrimage in late June or early July each year. The Abbey has also become a focal point for Christian renewal with large-scale events such as "Hearts on Fire" in July and a very successful evening of classical music in August, both of which attracted thousands of people. The latter was in part planned by Michael Eavis, who pioneered the massive pop festivals at nearby Pilton which have attracted up to 100,000 people. This change may not yet express unity in diversity, but the monopoly by one kind of spiritual expression has been broken, a welcome sign of repentance by the Christian Church, an indication of a reduction in Christian arrogance.

> The monopoly of one kind of spiritual expression has been broken, a welcome sign of reduction in Christian arrogance

Following the introduction of Christian welcomers and growth in both prayer and Christian healing at St John's, evening services of prayer and praise reach out to people for miles around. As a consequence Glastonbury has been much affected by "Toronto Blessings". This involves not only the traditionally "high" Anglican Church of St John's but the Free Churches and the Community Church, whose leaders hold strongly to evangelical Christian "fundamentals" and present a challenge to spiritually dormant churches and Alternatives and attract members from other churches. Perhaps St Paul was right when he said, "All things work together for good." It is more productive to learn how to relate to "fundamentalists" of whatever kind than to condemn "fundamentalism".

Whilst it is not spiritually healthy for the Church to become too closely involved with party politics, the arrival on the Glastonbury scene of a Residents Association, rejecting both the Conservative and Liberal Democrat positions, at first led to a hardening of attitudes to unemployed and homeless people, especially the 16–25 age group, and above all towards "travellers", all of whom tend to be regarded as being addicted to drink and drugs — a threat to be scapegoated. Since a number of young people have died, attitudes are beginning to change for the better, not only in the churches but at district and county level. Locally a meeting at the Town Hall between councillors and church members revealed that some councillors objected to the provision of sandwiches to those who were hungry, let alone to the excellent hot meal provided twice a month on Sundays at St Benedict's church hall. A Conservative councillor made it clear that the churches have a duty to care for those who are deprived. Public opinion has moved to some extent against government policy which treats people as outlaws rather than human beings — a Criminal Justice Act has been passed which reminds us of Robin Hood and the Sheriff of Nottingham. Locally hardliners are destroying their own case — they need courage. The rest of us need compassion for them if they are to be helped to climb down from positions which expose lack of charity to those in genuine need.

> We need compassion for hardliners if they are to be helped to climb down from their positions

In November for the first time members of the churches,

including clergy and ministers (not just James), met with councillors, social workers and Alternatives and representatives of the Friends and Families of Travellers (a national organization with headquarters in Glastonbury) at the Assembly Rooms. A steering committee was formed to bring to the birth a much-needed day centre in the town. This may stem in part from meetings held in the Town Hall under the auspices of the Mendip Council for Voluntary Services. Dawn is beginning to come to Glastonbury, even if there is still blind opposition to providing emergency sites for travellers near Glastonbury and elsewhere in the county. Toleration in Somerset is growing, which could mean that provision may eventually be made for those who live in benders and caravans. The battle is not yet won.

Since its formation three years ago, the Quest Community has been under immense pressure. The small number of members have sought to help those who suffer homelessness and unemployment and struggle with personal difficulties, mental illness, and addiction to drink and drugs. The community seeks to develop a Christian spirituality which reaches out to the Christ within many Alternatives without antagonizing traditional denominational churchgoers too much. A very few beds have been provided near the centre of Glastonbury, as happened on a larger scale in the early and mid-1980s at Greenlands Farm before the Assembly Rooms became the main centre in Glastonbury where care was provided for the poor by Alternatives.

> Quest seeks a Christian spirituality which reaches out to the Christ within many Alternatives

If there can be an effective link between the evangelical revival with its enthusiasm, between those who care for the poor and the deprived, and those who value universal "catholic" faith to which many in our denominational churches aspire, the relevance of the Christian faith to the contemporary world should increase. As the Celtic saints of old knew, humility, patience and love are of the essence of a Christianity which transcends class and national boundaries and avoids schism.

Celtic spirituality

After meeting the late Revd Martin Reith some years ago, when he was a priest-hermit in the Episcopal Church of Scotland despite his strong Presbyterian roots, a pilgrimage was planned to Iona. This took place in 1991, not all that long before his death. The requested follow-up pilgrimage was made to Whitby, Durham, Jarrow and Lindisfarne during 1994. Fr Reith's knowledge of our Christian, druidic and pagan roots, his awareness of God as Lord of History, of Christ in creation, of the One God in Trinity, and of Celtic awareness of ancient as well as of modern science, made for a refreshing wholeness in his theology. Here lie roots of a truly "catholic" spirituality not under the authority of Rome. During 1996 James and Rosemary led a pilgrimage to Wales to explore and to learn from Welsh spirituality.

These roots give rise to a Celtic understanding of the role of King as sharing in the suffering of his people (as did King George VI). This means leadership which serves, and community without that conflict between hierarchy and grassroots which still plagues all denominations (not just the C of E and the RC Church). If there is a deeper awareness of this amongst Scots and Welsh the time is coming ripe for this to penetrate darkest England; the time is "set for the fall and rising again of many in Israel" as it was when Christ Jesus came into the world for the first time to usher in a new understanding of the nature of God and of authority. The third pilgrimage to Wales gave pilgrims an opportunity to explore these underlying roots, which are also to be found in the west of England, including Glastonbury, where they have surfaced mostly outside the church amongst Alternatives. Inevitably this is far from popular amongst those who support the status quo, who place a high value on materialism supported by party and denominational theologies, and find unity in diversity difficult if not impossible.

There was not much unity when St Augustine met Welsh

bishops within a few years of his arrival in AD597. At Aust in 1996 the pilgrims met the Anglican woman priest-in-charge, her Anglican churchwarden and his wife, a "cradle" Catholic who had taken the initiative by bringing us together. Her Roman Catholic base was secure enough to enable her to reach out towards that unity in service and diversity near the heart of the Celtic Christian tradition. We were starting to learn that those who maintain that the Celtic and Roman traditions are totally opposed or totally identical are misinformed. This view was strengthened when we moved to Llantwit Major and met St Cadoc, St Illtyd and St Samson through the good offices of the rector and his wife, together with the local Roman Catholic priest, who brought us into contact with the 5th- and 6th-century roots of Welsh community life, as well as with individual hermits.

> Unity in service and diversity is near the heart of the Celtic Christian tradition

At Whitland some of us met Hywel the Good, a contemporary of St Dunstan, who framed laws after consulting the Welsh people. After centuries of oppression this tradition resurfaced early in the 15th century during the revolt by Owen Glendower, who obtained the backing of the Avignon Pope against English and Roman domination but was ruthlessly crushed. Five hundred years later England has begun to learn that the consequence has been our own diminishment as well as division in Britain. The Welsh nationalist rector of Pennal, near Machynlleth, played a major role in illuminating us and we became aware that the tradition of dissent at the heart of the Welsh tradition is still alive in the Church in Wales and — when necessary — kicking! This dissent is at the root of the Christian spiritual revival associated with the building of the Welsh chapels in the 18th and 19th centuries. At St David's we learnt that chapels there were all built with their backs to the cathedral because of persecution by Christians who held positions of power locally in Church and State. Since the disestablishment of the Church in Wales the situation has begun to improve as the grip of England on the spiritual, political and cultural life of Wales has weakened.

At St David's Cathedral the diocesan system inherited from Rome is still favoured. At Walton West we met a priest with a strong local congregation who looks to *peregrini* or wandering hermits for inspiration. Perhaps these two traditions are not mutually exclusive but together can make for unity in diversity and live together in mutual respect and trust — which was impossible when St Augustine came to Aust or during English attempts to destroy Welsh culture and language.

Further journeying to Tywyn revealed more insights into Welsh community life. A visit to Pont Robert in Powys, where there is a remarkable ecumenical centre, unveiled the importance of grassroots Christian theology as expressed by an "uneducated" farmer's nonconformist daughter. Ann Griffiths lived two hundred years ago and wrote both hymns and poems. Scholars now compare her to Mother Julian of Norwich; she might also be compared with some of the Biblical prophetesses. On to Pennant Melangell, where the restored shrine attracts many people to a remote valley, now as in former centuries. So does Holywell, a Roman Catholic shrine not suppressed at the Reformation, perhaps because it was built with funds provided by the grandmother of King Henry VIII. At Criccieth, through the kindness of the archdeacon of Merioneth and his wife, we discovered more of a wonderful poetic tradition which bridges the class gulf in that land of hope and glory which is Wales. The pilgrimage ended on the north coast, where links were made with St Beuno, present-day Jesuits, Gerard Manley Hopkins, and the Roman Catholic tradition with its immense spiritual riches. Some of us visited nearby St Asaph, also associated with St Kentigern, in an area where Welsh, Irish, Pictish and English traditions meet and enrich each other.

The pilgrimage helped us realize how impoverished is our spirituality which knows little or nothing of Welsh, Scottish, Cornish and Irish saints

The pilgrimage helped to make us realize how impoverished is a British spirituality which knows little or nothing of Welsh, Scottish, Cornish and Irish saints. Perhaps it takes the way of Jesus Mediator to bring these differing insights together, to enable us to meet at the foot of the Cross to resolve such conflicts as that over authority, which still bedevils relationships between Rome, Canterbury and the Free Churches — let alone the Alternatives, who look at us and see arrogance rather than the person of Jesus the Christ, and the desire to control rather than to serve.

If Welsh hospitality is a major memory of the pilgrimage, it became clear that unity cannot come where there is no more than a papering-over of the cracks, by paving the way for a vast administrative machine for the whole Church, or by surrender to those who insist on a stringent moral code which alienates rather than makes people holy. Perhaps hope for the future depends upon our accepting all that is good and of God in our pagan and druidic roots, which bring respect for the sacredness of the earth and for creation and knowing the Trinity in Unity, as revealed both by the incarnate Jesus who is also Christ, the cosmic Christ of creation. Not only our Celtic forebears but Red Indians, African and Aboriginal peoples in many parts of the world held or still hold to truth we in Europe have largely lost — so do some of those on the spiritual journey in the Middle East and in Asia. All truth needs to be sifted in the light of the person of Jesus the Christ. Maybe the way this can be done is to explore Family Tree Ministry.

Family tree ministry

For centuries the Church in England has neglected the person and role of Christ in creation, stressing his role in forgiving and redeeming individuals from the power of sin; this was seen in very limited terms. Not only our God but our Christ Jesus has been too small, and we have been blind to passing on an inferior quality of life by previous generations to their descendants, who have suffered much from the failure of the Church in Britain. If our Christian spirituality has its shortcomings, so has that of other faiths. In India the Hindu doctrine of karma and reincarnation has been the means of keeping the poor, especially the Untouchables, in a state of subjection. Not only Brahmans but Christians who accept Jesus as Saviour or Mary as Mother of God can become a false spiritual elite. Jews and Muslims, all of us, can and do follow the same route. Perhaps Family Tree Ministry can help us deal with false spiritual roots and purify the Christian Church and other faiths when Christ Jesus imparts deeper levels of forgiveness, adding not only more true light but glory as well.

Family Tree Ministry, as practised by people like Dr Kenneth McAll, has revealed as a result of his experience in China, that the Old Testament view that the sins of parents are visited on their children "unto the third and fourth generation" is true. The sin of inter-racial conflict goes deeper than that, as Ireland and Bosnia bear witness. Children with parents, grandparents, ancestors, of differing national and spiritual traditions suffer physical or mental breakdown caused by deep inner conflicts; their personalities need reintegrating. For some generations this may not be important, but the time comes when such conflicts need healing if a future generation is to become whole — more like Christ Jesus. For a great many people that time is *now*, and a deeper, richer deliverance is at hand connected with the Kingdom of God. A conference at Abbey House, Glastonbury, began to explore such questions with the help of Kenneth McAll and the Revd Russ Parker. Kenneth McAll made it clear that he believes that spirits exist before conception, and it is likely that he believes in reincarnation as well. The time was not ripe for this to be pursued but it is evident that a major challenge to the limitations of Western religion and science is on the way.

Two hundred years ago during the French Revolution, when the rational part of human nature was becoming dominant, the time was coming ripe for the shackles by which the Church used its authority to prevent scientific investigation to be thrown off. This led to great advances in the light of increased knowledge; these advances are now being superseded. Empirical natural science is having to make room for psychic and spiritual dimensions if it is to be relevant, uniting rather

> The saying that sins of parents are visited on their children 'unto the third and fourth generation' is true

than dividing. This should pave the way for the One God, who creates and redeems, to be seen once again to integrate all science and all truth, earthly and heavenly, in one order; whether we like it or not, all sciences and all religious faiths have to be prepared to relate to each other.

Jesus came to bear witness to truth, not deny it. When the Church comes to terms with this explosion, theology may once again be the Queen of Sciences, which at present it is patently not. More rigid Christians and third-rate scientists will find this hard, for it means that principalities and powers at the natural and psychic level can no longer be regarded as being subject to inadequate belief in Christ or treated as outgrown and dismissed.

Theology may once again be the Queen of Sciences — rigid Christians and third-rate scientists will find this hard

To be redeemed by Christ in the world to which we are moving, we need to commit ourselves to a much greater Christ Jesus, who is big enough to embrace truth for which Alternatives stand — all those spiritually inclined or dedicated to scientific investigation.

For some Christians this already means that astrology, the powers associated with the sun, the moon and the stars and the signs of the zodiac, regarded by many as dubious and even dangerous, need to be brought under the authority of Christ. This is a mystical relationship; in no way does it restore the right of the Church to have control, but to serve as Jesus served and gave spiritual leadership on earth — as he does now when we are in tune with Him and with God. Third-rate science and third-rate religion, which puts God in a box to suit theological or scientific prejudice dressed up as truth, may die hard, as did that of hidebound scribes and Pharisees two thousand years ago, but die they must. The time has come for the human race to grow up spiritually, as increased knowledge and inter-communication is thrusting us into a deep surging sea. To some this means a "New Age" is coming; to others this new age started with Jesus, his apostles and the early Celtic saints, to whom family tree ministry was part of their practice and discipline based on spiritual awareness.

Today as places like Iona, Whitby, centres in Wales,

Cornwall and Ireland, and Glastonbury in England discover their role, we will be enabled to rediscover, as did Fr Martin Reith, the meaning of the word "catholic" aligned with the truly catholic faith as held in the 5th and 6th centuries in Britain — related to Rome but not under the authority of Rome. This rediscovery will set a successor of John Paul II free to be bishop of Rome as John Paul I is believed to have planned; in addition all of us will be set free to follow Jesus as we render unto Caesar that which is Caesar's — in both Church and State — and unto God that which belongs to God. The fullness of Christ-centred family tree ministry can help resolve the contemporary crisis over authority which splits the Church, making for Episcopal and Presbyterian forms of church government, schisms between Christians and lack of respect for truths held by those of other faiths.

Truly 'catholic' faith as held in Celtic Britain: related to Rome but not under Rome

New communities and the churches in Glastonbury

1996 brought to Glastonbury Fr Ray Simpson of the ecumenical community of Aidan and Hilda, who is now based on Lindisfarne. He seeks to restore to England the Celtic and catholic dimension which gets lost when power is abused. This fruitful visit stemmed from contact with the Revd Russ Parker, one of the trustees of the community. A link has been made between Fr Simpson and the infant Quest Community in Glastonbury led by the Revd John Sumner, which is seeking to build bridges between the churches and spiritually-minded Alternatives (including travellers and the dispossessed) attracted to Glastonbury. A magazine, *Glastonbury Thorn*, is periodically circulated, which it is hoped will supersede this newsletter. The discipline of the Aidan and Hilda community has much to offer the Quest Community and Glastonbury churches as we come to grips with changes being thrust upon us if an adequate prayer life and discipline are to emerge in Glastonbury.

One sign of local readiness for change already mentioned is the 1997 ecumenical pilgrimage from Rome to Derry

(Londonderry). Beyond this, the millennium provides a much greater opportunity for spiritual progress as the Church in England comes together for celebrations and also explores our role as a nation in relation to Europe, the Commonwealth, the USA and the rest of the world as part of creation, visible and invisible, in which Jesus, the cosmic Christ of creation and redemption in human flesh, embraces the whole of science and religion — earth and heaven — in one order.

The world scene

More than 1500 years ago Europe was torn by invasions and conflicts between east and west and between north and south, which developed into a struggle between Catholicism, Orthodoxy and Protestantism. There are those who wish to forget, even to forgive and forget, the past. South Africa, emerging from the horrors of apartheid, reveals there is a better way — to remember in the light of the Cross with its pain so that forgiveness becomes more complete, restoring more abundant life. In this way the principalities and powers associated with the symbols of the beast and the dragon in the Bible become subject to the authority of Christ.

> Remember in the light of the Cross with its pain — forgiveness is more complete, restoring more abundant life

A prophetic Protestant strand of theology from the USA, which at one time regarded the Soviet Union as the modern equivalent of the beast or dragon of the Revelation of St John the Divine, warns that the European Community has now taken over this role. It is not necessary to believe this extreme teaching but it makes sense to acknowledge that Mammon (materialism) is a major force in Europe, even in the churches. Many who have experienced the presence of angels, and those who relate to saints and spirits, have found no help from clergy and have been condemned; such experience is regarded as satanic; many have as a consequence left the churches, which have failed to "test the spirits whether they are of God". Perhaps that is why what is happening in Africa is so important, for there is much in Africa similar to our deep spiritual roots in Britain. It is revealed as we explore relationship with ancestors;

deep hurts and sins of previous generations, such as damage to souls in war through battle, murder and sudden death, can be forgiven and healed, and unquiet or earthbound spirits are freed and laid to rest. Then the Kingdom of God can come.

In this country there is a deeply held conviction that our role in the world is to withstand tyranny whatever the cost to ourselves in blood, toil, tears and sweat. This is at the heart of our political and religious tradition. When party politics and theology take over with futile arguments, we cease listening to one another. We have not been without our prophets. In the last war God raised up Winston Churchill and Aneurin Bevan. In the 1970s Enoch Powell and Tony Benn were perhaps truer prophets than Edward Heath, who sold us out to Europe — a sale which has cost billions, and even now we have not paid the full price. When spiritual values came to the fore in days gone by, we were able to overcome the might of France and Spain backed by the Papacy. It is our national and spiritual tradition to mediate between extremes, a role we still endeavour to follow in our relationship with Europe. Where opposites are reconciled — in science, in politics and in religion — the way to spiritual progress opens up. This brings us to paradox and above all to overcoming the principalities and powers of evil in the light and glory of the supreme paradox of Cross and Resurrection, which is in the sacred heart of God and of creation.

> Britain's national and spiritual tradition is to mediate between extremes, a role we still try to follow in our relationship with Europe

Finally, one person in a unique position to make a special contribution in the early years of the new millennium is HRH Prince Charles, in some ways despised and rejected, whose insights and vocation can help us in Britain so that we cease to be a kingdom divided against itself. We need to be united with a clearer spiritual vision of our future role as a nation in no way subsidiary to a self-centred European federal community or a community of nation states. We can be a nation destined not to rule but to serve, in the light of the Cross and Resurrection of Him who is not only Saviour King and Lord but Mediator. This is not a comfortable vocation, but it provides an interpretation of the Christian faith and the Bible which can help us meet the challenge which the next thousand years will throw at us. Clergy and laity of the Church in England together need to prepare to meet that challenge, just as Rome rose to the challenge of inevitable overthrow through St Augustine of Hippo and his City of God. For us in Britain, as we cease to be at the heart of a world empire and a world power, there is a different destiny, to be a blessing to the world. Surely that is a worthwhile role for a nation and for the Christian Church in these islands.

As we cease to be a world empire Britain has a different destiny: to be a blessing to the world

January 1998

Fourteenth Glastonbury Newsletter

In January 1997 it was hoped that further Turnbull newsletters from Glastonbury would be unnecessary. But there were issues in danger of going by default, hence this final attempt to reach some of those who wish to see Glastonbury as a potential focal point for reconciliation, as the Christian Church in Britain learns how to relate creatively to those of other faiths at a time of change in our relationship with Parliament, the Monarchy and the Commonwealth, with Europe, including the Papacy, and the rest of the world — with mystical and spiritual dimensions ignored by materialist rationalist theologians and scientists, to their impoverishment and ours. When knowledge becomes separated from wisdom and insight there may be considerable short-term progress, but arrogant technological "experts" with little or no sense of spiritual purpose lead to long-term complications and tangles. Simplicity is at the heart of real progress.

In a materialist society disintegration grows; deep questions are kept at arm's length by recourse to medically prescribed drugs, to dependence on tobacco, alcohol, cannabis and the motorcar, to criminal marketing of "hard drugs"; many become victims. Behind "yuppies" are "fat cats" given to sleaze, who milk the system and, like drugged-up artists or sports stars, are near or over the edge of criminality. Only those who have a concern for peace or the environment, as do some Christians and members of CND or Greenpeace, have a strong enough sense of purpose to stand firm and face the odium inspired by sections of the press. Inevitably some of the poor, the homeless, and those who suffer turn to violence which, as in Ireland, appears to be the only way to make governments listen. Secrecy and hypocrisy are, however, features of not only party politics and third-rate science; we are all prone to forget that we too are at fault. The day of judgement is approaching.

> In a materialist society disintegration grows; deep questions are kept at arm's length by recourse to drugs and the motorcar

Progress through conflict

In 1979, faced with the prospect of left-wing dictatorship or chaos, the British electorate opted for Margaret Thatcher. Faced with tendencies towards right-wing fascism for 18 years, the same electorate opted for New Labour on 1 May 1997. The die is cast for far-reaching change, which many will not like, though the tragic death of Princess Diana revealed the quest for a more caring society. Both political and religious conflict lies ahead. Such conflict is still around in Glastonbury but — because of our history — Glastonbury has begun once again to make a spiritual contribution, both nationally and internationally. The mere existence of the Quest Community, very much in the front line and learning to be a community, has helped to encourage others within and outside of the churches towards cooperation. During 1997 the Quest Community faced a crisis. One cause was the demand for hospitality and an ever-open door for those with deep needs, before theological issues had been adequately faced; it proved that Quest had an inadequate base for sustained growth. In the town and denominational churches, some, reluctant to come to terms with change, see Quest as a threat rather than providing spiritual inspiration. There is inevitable tension between those who see the future in terms of One Inclusive Great Church and those who value exclusive denominations with their partial truths, whether Roman, Anglican, Evangelical or Free Church.

Nevertheless in Glastonbury as in Britain, the churches, or parts of them, are beginning to make a stand. So are some of the Alternatives, and that is what this postscript is about.

Inter-faith cooperation

It should come as no surprise that some considered the Quest Community was on the way out during 1997. The hope is that 1998 will see the emergence of a community with more corporate leadership, trusting in God as members continue to hammer out a genuine ecumenical Christian presence related to Alternatives, in a town which cannot fulfil its role for the next millennium until the need for further change is accepted. Seen in that light, 1997 has been a year of progress, even if Quest has its faults and reactionary elements in and outside of the churches use that as excuse for opposition. In any society, powerful characters get a following for what they propose until people see the flaws in their arguments and find a better way; during such times people get hurt — not for nothing did Jesus say, "Father, forgive them for they know not what they do." Glastonbury of its nature and history tends to look for scapegoats, and yet, through their suffering, the community benefits in the long run.

During 1997 the Quest Community was not the only scapegoat; another example was the Robert Barton Trust. Opposition to a proposed day centre came to a climax when a coachload of protesters went to a meeting at the Mendip District Council office in Shepton Mallet and shouted down speakers who were gently and quietly making a case for facilities to be provided in Glastonbury for a measure of daycare for single parents and their children, for young local unemployed and homeless people in need. Partly through this, the spiritual eyes and ears of some of those who had swallowed the propaganda of extremists for the last twenty-five years have been opened. Years of effort at the Gothic Image, the Chalice Well, Greenlands Farm, the Assembly Rooms, Children's World and the Glastonbury Experience have not been in vain. The quest for the Holy Grail is on; churches and Alternatives are beginning to cooperate together.

The Abbey and pilgrimage

At long last the Abbey has begun to fulfil a more prominent role. "Hearts on Fire" has catered for evangelical Christians and now the genius of Michael Eavis, who founded the local pop festival of international fame, led to a Classical Extravaganza within the Abbey grounds attracting many people. Prior to such events spiritual plays have been performed in the Abbey to very small audiences, even if their standard has been high. Also on a very small scale is Tuesday worship in St Patrick's or St Joseph's Chapels, which touch only a handful of people, nearly all Anglicans, at a time when a growing number of people look to the Abbey as a centre for spiritual endeavour going back to pre-Christian times. The Abbey faces the danger of being accused of catering only for the well-to-do who can afford high prices. In addition, annual pilgrimages can perpetuate and even aggravate the divisions of the past, as happens with the June pilgrimage, which fails to honour the "two integrities" as agreed by the Church of England [regarding ordination of women]; this attitude undermines the Christian witness of the Abbey, especially to those outside the Church. Some of those who feel shut out have turned to hate both Church and Abbey, and of this Christians need to take note.

... the Abbey as a centre for spiritual endeavour going back to pre-Christian times

During 1997 it became possible for Glastonbury to be included on a small spur to the main pilgrimage from Canterbury to Derry (Londonderry). This helped to bring local churches together even if there was "no room at the inn" for Alternatives, who would have valued some form of participation. Perhaps the millennium will give an opportunity to break free of 16th-century attitudes which still hold local churches in bondage? Christians Together in Glastonbury are seeking to wait upon God and have a concern for contemplative prayer, as practised by religious orders and bodies like the Society of Friends, as a basis for future action.

Other initiatives

During 1997 the University of Avalon (now known as the Avalon Foundation), centred on the Glastonbury Experience, launched a project, which other Alternatives were also considering, for an "all faiths" sanctuary to be sited preferably in the Abbey grounds. Attempts are being made to seek a creative relationship with churches; joint groups have begun meeting to find a spiritual base for cooperation and to plan future events. Both local people and people from outside Glastonbury, some known nationally and internationally, are involved. This is still at an early stage.

Mendip District Council, with the establishment of a local "task force" which relates to the town council, the Chamber of Commerce, churches and Alternatives, has begun to make an impression. A town-centre officer has been appointed to encourage initiatives, including a tourism forum. Partly through Chalice Well trustees, a "pilgrimage forum" is in the offing, which could help the churches and Alternatives break free of hangovers from 16th-century attitudes, which split the Church in England into warring segments and cause Christians to be on the fringe of local life rather than at its heart.

... could help break free of hangovers from 16th-century attitudes

The Roman Catholic Church, which suffered a devastating blow some years ago when its school was sold, depriving it of premises, has been able to build one of the best church halls in the town for Church and community activities. St John's Anglican Church bought and converted a small local workshop into a new church centre designed for community outreach; this followed increasing use of the Church for prayer-and-praise services on Sunday evenings twice a month, and also for meeting visitors to the town, social outreach, and Christian healing. There has also been spiritual growth at St Benedict's Anglican Church, where the church hall — much improved — is helping to provide meals on Sundays at minimum cost as a service to the community.

As a result of initiative from the United Reformed Church,

a new relationship is developing not only with the Methodist Church but also with St Benedict's; this is unity in worship and in practice. An initiative begun some years ago on a small scale in the new community hall on Windmill Hill by the URC has now grown into an ecumenical venture with regular weekly Christian worship. There are many people on Windmill Hill, which consists in the main of a large (by Glastonbury standards) council estate where there are few community activities. Many residents have little respect for the Christian Church; some have good reason to be angry, and hatred is not unknown. This attempt to atone for past failures shows courage; change in attitudes will not come easily.

There is now a productive Orthodox Christian presence in the High Street, with both a shop and a chapel. This is led by Father John Ives, a former Anglican priest who with his wife Thelma (now ordained as an Orthodox deaconess) has joined the Celtic Orthodox Church centred on an abbey in France. This can help the whole Church in Glastonbury and Alternatives to draw on wider and deeper spiritual roots. There is still need to recover the Celtic roots here and in the Abbey which enable the Church to relate worship to the daily working lives of people and to the nearness of the Communion of Saints, to paradise and heaven — where there is no vision the people perish.

> There is still need to recover the Celtic roots which enable the Church to relate worship to the daily working lives of people — and to the nearness of the Communion of Saints

The link is growing with the Community of Aidan and Hilda, founded as an ecumenical order by Father Ray Simpson, now based on Lindisfarne and reaching out to both Britain and Ireland. This link-up came through the Acorn Christian Healing Trust, founded by Bishop Morris Maddocks when assistant bishop in the Anglican diocese of Bath and Wells. This ecumenical trust is now under the leadership of the Revds Russ Parker and Michael Mitton, who are concerned not just with the renewal of "sick" individuals but with healing of communities and the land. Perhaps the day is coming nearer when people in Glastonbury will be ready for that strand of spirituality expressed by Brian Frost (amongst other concerns he is a Methodist lay preacher) who wrote *Glastonbury Journey*, about an unknown Glastonbury mystic, Marjorie Milne, in 1986. Since then he has written *The Politics of Forgiveness*, a biography of Lord Soper, and his new book, *Struggling to Forgive*, about Truth and Reconciliation in South Africa, is due to be published in June 1998. Brian is concerned with healing the soul of nations, including Britain and Ireland. Even if Glastonbury is slowly coming to terms with such insights, the quest for true community will be long and hard. There is much to be done by the Quest Community and others in Glastonbury if we are to become a focal point for reconciliation.

When the Spirit comes

Churches Together in Somerset have begun to get their act together; there are plans for an event on Glastonbury Tor in May 1998 which relates Jubilee 2000 to forgiving the debts of desperately poor nations. Perhaps this is another sign of the coming of the Spirit of God. When the Spirit comes to the churches, Christians are set free from barren arguments by hardline evangelical, Protestant, Roman Catholic or middle-of-the-road Christians who become politicized and polarized and refuse to listen to those — including Alternatives — who see different areas of truth and different ways of communicating the One Gospel. We cannot live by bread alone or by the Evangelical Word or the Social Gospel, we need (as Jesus taught) every word that proceeds out of the mouth of God. Some of those words come through Jews, Muslims, Hindus, Buddhists and Alternatives.

The soul of Glastonbury, like the soul of Britain and the whole world, cries out for healing. For many of us that means the Church in England learning to be humble enough to listen to other sections of the One Holy Catholic and Apostolic Church and to those alienated and outside. When that happens, the mutual anathematizing and cursing, which stems from the Reformation and from the destruction of the early Celtic

Christian Church, will be a thing of the past and people will once again say, "See how these Christians love one another." If Christians Together and the Quest Community help us find the way to that, as Marjorie Milne did in the 1960s and 1970s, and as Greenlands Farm, the Alternatives and the Assembly Rooms did in the 1980s, the Christian Church may yet play the role which Glastonbury needs, drawing from all sections of our society — as we follow in the footsteps of Jesus, who was nailed to the Cross, died, was buried and rose again to enable us to find the way to life and the healing of the nations as we look to the millennium and beyond.

People will once again say: 'See how these Christians love one another'

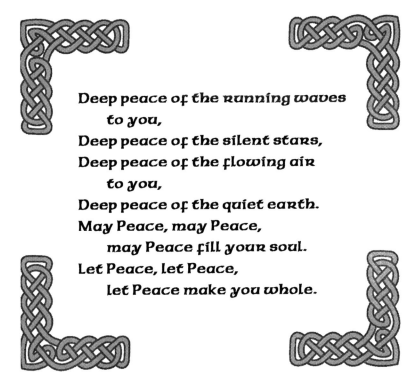

Deep peace of the running waves
   to you,
Deep peace of the silent stars,
Deep peace of the flowing air
   to you,
Deep peace of the quiet earth.
May Peace, may Peace,
   may Peace fill your soul.
Let Peace, let Peace,
   let Peace make you whole.

Appendix

Considering Celtic roots on Iona

by James Turnbull

reprinted from the October 1991 issue of *Health and Healing*,
the bimonthly magazine of the Churches' Council for Health and Healing
(St Marylebone Parish Church, Marylebone Road, London, NW1 5LT)

The changing scene

As knowledge increases even more rapidly and higher education becomes more common, there is growing ferment in natural science as well as in theology and philosophy. The day of ever more strident rational analysis has run its course. Psychology, sociology and parapsychology, technology associated with electricity, electromagnetism and computers, as well as mathematics and linguistics are thrusting us into new dimensions following the splitting of the atom and emergence of nuclear physics.

In the past these areas of knowledge have been seen as entirely separate from one another and from God; now they are seen as relating to the One God who inspires them all and much more besides. This means that the Church has to learn how to relate to the whole of life with its paradoxes and opposites and that we need to take more account of intuition, music and art, which have often been viewed with suspicion. The Churches' Council for Health and Healing through its magazine is perhaps well placed to explore this new relationship. It is concerned with healing not just of sick individuals but with healing all people into communion with God, respecting science, the earth and the whole creation.

The belief that the key to tackling this situation lies in the spirituality of the early Celtic Christian Church led to the planning of a small conference which took place on Iona from June 1 to 8 in 1991. It called for a recognition of the spiritual understanding of the Celts, much of which has been lost following the Inquisition, the Reformation and the French Revolution. Now in this age this lost truth is re-emerging.

Contact with our Celtic inheritance

The small conference was an attempt to open the way for English Christians to learn to draw on the immense spiritual riches which enabled many saints of the early Celtic Church to meet the deepest needs of many individuals and communities. They included such people as St Ninian, St Patrick, St Bridget, St Cuthbert and a host of others known and unknown. Some were connected with Glastonbury; all shared a sense of the harmony between earth and heaven, the natural and the spiritual expressing itself in a respect for the animal kingdom as well as a regard for the earth and all life as sacred. All related the person of Jesus the Christ to all that was good in the mystery religions of the day, at the same time fighting the powers of darkness that they encountered. Twelve priests or ministers and twelve lay Christians, twelve men and twelve women from different parts of the country came together on Iona for a week to be open to Celtic insights into universal truth in Christ. Different levels of knowledge and experience were open to one another. All were stretched; all had much to learn.

Early Celtic spirituality

Early Celtic Christianity related the outer to the inner; the physical, the psychic, the spiritual and celestial realms were seen as part of a whole; this enabled integrated people to face the open sea of life with its powers, monsters and dragons; the way of communication becomes picture language, parable and story, rather than abstract truth. New light, new life and glory opens up as poetry, music, storytelling and artistic talent gives rise to the Book of Kells and the Lindisfarne Gospels and to more complete sacramental worship. Here revelations of hidden truths are not evils to be fought and subjugated but new knowledge to be applied with wisdom and insight by leaders who serve people. In bringing everything to Christ, people are made whole, sexuality is hallowed and directed aright and not repressed, the whole earth is made fertile and healed. Is this not like the golden age of the kingdom of God coming on earth as in heaven, for which many long as we seek as best as we can to break free from the powers of darkness and roots of spiritual disorder?

Contemporary spiritual disorder

As we apply these insights to our contemporary situation we learn that neglect of our Celtic inheritance gives rise to a host of barren arguments and discussion. When life and religion are allowed to drift apart, when greed, status and division exist in society and the Church, secularism begins to take over. Until the Church gives priority to overcoming the principalities and powers of the universe — including the power of Mammon which divides rich from poor — nation will continue to be set against nation, class against class, black against white and men against women. Those who live fat will defend themselves against the rapidly multiplying millions of the Third World; we opt for increasing violence, more fear and anxiety, all signs of sickness of soul and spirit.

On Iona we learned that there is a rich Celtic spiritual inheritance to draw on from Scotland, Ireland, Wales and further afield for all who are open to truth. This inheritance is not for those satisfied with fundamentalist religion, which reflects more of Old Testament Law than the New Covenant, but is for those willing to be thrust into the open sea.

The cost of fundamentalism

It should be noted that it is alien to Celtic spirituality to condemn fundamentalists like those who seek to persuade members of Parliament to pass legislation which reminds some of us of the Inquisition, witchcraft trials and terrible injustices in the past which caused millions of deaths. It does expose threats of hellfire and damnation which are behind a false spirituality designed to enforce obedience; it opposes aggression against innocent people who are prayed against as satanic and possessed by demons when they may be the modern equivalent of the common people who heard Jesus gladly. Without proper correction, fundamentalism becomes denial of truth and causes endless suffering.

The effect of the Iona conference

In this light those who took part in the week on Iona found that caring and acceptance of each other — truth, heresies and all — made for growth, renewal and more wholeness; we learnt to wash each other's feet in the patience, humility and love of Celtic monks. In this perhaps lies hope of a new partnership between religion and science as both change, and we prepare to walk in the footsteps of Jesus like the early Christian Celts, but related to contemporary life. This seemed to make it possible for Presbyterian and Episcopalian, for Roman Catholic, Anglican and Free Church person, for Scot, Welsh and Irish, even Southern English, to come together and be as members of one family or subtribe, so that we can face a sick troubled world together. We share a common faith in Christ Jesus, God in human flesh, crucified risen and ascended, who comes to renew the Church, to empower us to meet the challenge from other faiths and to share the Gospel with those who value the New Age; we accept that, through them, God may be reminding us of truths the Church has forgotten, enabling us to grow beyond our present impoverished spirituality.

The conference on Iona enabled those taking part to give thanks for the re-emergence of Celtic Christian roots which can help us handle massive growth of scientific and spiritual truth. This means we can look at the future with courage and confidence (but not certainty) as we go forward under authority as we live by faith wherever Jesus may lead.

Bibliography

A few of James Turnbull's favourite books

John O'Donohue
Anam Cara: spiritual wisdom from the Celtic world
Bantam Press, 1997   ISBN 0 593 04201 8
Ray Simpson
Soul friendship: Celtic insights into spiritual mentoring
Hodder and Stoughton, 1990   0 340 73548 1
Dr Kenneth McAll
Healing the family tree
Sheldon Press, 1982   0 85969 364 3
Ian Bradley
The Celtic way
Darton, Longman and Todd, 1993   0 232 52001 1
Henry Drummond (1851–1897)
The greatest thing in the world
Collins   0 87516675 X
(Dozens of other editions. The text is also online: *www.ccel.org)*
William Temple
Readings in St John's Gospel
Macmillan, 1960   0 333 03148 2
Bede Griffiths
Return to the centre
Templegate   0 87243 112 6

Michael Ramsay
Be still and know: a study in the life of prayer
Cowley, 1993   1 5610 1083 9

Mother Mary Clare, SLG
Encountering the depths
SLG Press, 1993   0 72830 137 7

Brian Frost
Glastonbury journey: Marjorie Milne's search for reconciliation
Becket, 1986   0 7289 0023 8

Monica Furlong
Merton: a biography
SPCK, 1995   0 281 04871 1

Martin Reith
*Beyond the mountains: some Scottish studies in prayer and the
Church*
SPCK, 1979   0 281 03699 3

A. M. Allchin
*God's presence makes the world: the Celtic vision through the
centuries in Wales*
Darton, Longman and Todd, 1997   0 232 52206 5

Shirley Toulson
Celtic journeys in Scotland and the north of England
Fount, 1995   0 00 627882 5

Index

Some communities and religious orders

Ecumenical

Ammerdown Conference and Retreat Centre, Radstock, near Bath, Somerset, BA3 3BA; telephone (01761) 43 3709; centre@ammerdown.freeserve.co.uk

Community of Aidan and Hilda, The Open Gate, The Holy Island of Lindisfarne, Berwick-upon-Tweed, Northumberland, TD15 2SD; (01289) 38 9249 , www.aidan.org.uk (warden: Ray Simpson)

Grail Trust, The Liberty, Arthur's Gate, Montgomery, Powys, SY15 6QU; telephone (01686) 66 8502

Iona Community, Isle of Iona, Argyllshire, Scotland, PA76 6SN; telephone (01681) 70 0404

Lee Abbey, Lynton, Devon, EX35 6JL; telephone (01598) 75 2621

Pilsdon Community, Broadwindsor, near Bridport, Dorset, DT6 5NZ; telephone (01308) 86 8308

Quest Community at Glastonbury, 38 Magdalene Street, Glastonbury, Somerset, BA6 9EJ; telephone (01458) 83 5235; quest@fish.co.uk (leader: John Sumner)

Taizé Community, 71250 Taizé, France; telephone +33 3 85 50 30 02 (10h–12h, 17h–19h); www.taize.fr

Anglican

Society of St Francis, The Friary, Hilfield, Dorchester, Dorset, DT2 7BE; telephone (01300) 34 1345, email hilfieldssf@franciscans.org.uk

Community of St Francis, Compton Durville, South Petherton, Somerset, TA13 5ES; telephone (01460) 24 0473

Community of St Peter, St Peter's Convent, Maybury Hill, Woking, Surrey, GU22 8AE; telephone (01483) 76 1137

Community of the Resurrection, Mirfield, West Yorkshire, WF14 0DN; telephone (01924) 49 4318; www.mirfield.org.uk

Elmore Abbey, Church Lane, Speen, Newbury, Berkshire, RG14 1SA; telephone (01635) 3 3080 (formerly Nashdom Abbey. Anglican Benedictine. Abbot: Dom Basil Matthews, OSB)

Order of the Holy Paraclete, St Hilda's Priory, Sneaton Castle, Whitby, North Yorkshire, YO21 1RY; telephone (01947) 60 2079, email ohppriorywhitby@btinternet.com (prioress: Sister Judith, OHP)

Servants of the Will of God, Cuttinglye Lane, Crawley Down, Crawley, West Sussex, RH10 4LH

Sisters of the Love of God, Convent of the Incarnation, Fairacres, Oxford, OX4 1TB; telephone (01865) 71 1301 (Mother Rosemary, SLG)

Many of these have branch houses elsewhere in Britain and abroad. Go to http://orders.anglican.org/arcyb for an up-to-date list.

Roman Catholic

Buckfast Abbey, Buckfastleigh, Devon, TQ11 0EA; telephone (01364) 64 5500; www.buckfast.org.uk (Catholic Benedictine. Abbot: Anscar Vonier, OSB)

Downside Abbey, Stratton-on-the-Fosse, Radstock, Bath, Mendip, Somerset, BA3 4RH; telephone (01761) 23 5100; www.downside.co.uk (Roman Catholic Benedictine

Prinknash Abbey, Cranham, Painswick, Gloucester, GL4 8EX; telephone (01452) 81 2455

Other organizations

Acorn Christian Healing Trust, Whitehill Chase, High Street, Bordon, Hampshire, GU35 0AP; telephone (01420) 47 8121; www.acornchristian.org (director: Revd Russ Parker)

Churches' Council for Health and Healing (secretary), St Luke's Hospital for the Clergy, 14 Fitzroy Square, London, W1P 6AH; telephone (020) 7388 7903

Churches' Fellowship for Psychical and Spiritual Studies, The Rural Workshop, South Road, North Somercotes, nr Louth, Lincolnshire, LN11 7PT; www.cfpss.freeserve.co.uk

Guild of Health, Edward Wilson House, 26 Queen Anne Street, London, W1M 9LB; (020) 7580 2492 (general secretary: Revd Antonia Lynn)

Servants of Christ the King (secretary), Well Cottage, The Street, Kilmington, Axminster, Devon, EX13 7RW; (01297) 3 4142

The Prophetic Role of Glastonbury

*Readers are invited to respond to James Turnbull's newsletters.
Please write or email the Abbey Press address on page 4.
Responses will be collated and posted on the internet at
www.abbeypress.net/turnbull.htm*